MW00977462

The Father's Enduring Love

Evangeline Mae Fedor

PRESS

www.xulonpress.com

ACKNOWLEDGMENTS

To all who delight in the glory of God's promises as they are revealed to us in the Word of God, and to the Lord, Himself that He may be glorified through it all. The author has been blessed to have many friends and family walk with her on this journey in the past year as she has been revising and editing and making additions to her first publication of the book entitled "Embracing His Phrases."

A special thanks my dear family for responding to daily messages by saying that they "got it". It has been so good to hear from them regularly.

To Mary Marie Fedor, my heartfelt thanks for her inspiration as she gave her encouraging comments. She has contributed much joy for her attentive interest as she reviewed the manuscript.

To a very special friend, Bible scholar, and prayer partner, Marge Kvern, for introducing me to the devotional journal, "My Utmost for His Highest" by Oswald Chambers, which has been a special time of devotion to the Lord daily to enter two-line poems for the past 10 years.

To our dear granddaughter, Sheri Golla for her assistance in making the manuscript ready for publishing. She has been and still is a blessing in many ways.

To my dear friend, Marva Sheriff, an artist with a growing business at (www.credodesignsltd.com). She designed the cover.

To my wonderful husband, Peter, for his patience and support and sacrifice of time and companionship. He is good in the highest degree.

Most of all, I am thankful to the Lord Jesus Christ, who has made it possible to know Him personally. What an awesome God we have! He enhances our lives with His enduring love.

God, the Father
the Son
and the Holy Spirit

This book is dedicated to our very precious four children:

Steven Leroy Fedor
Suzanne Kathleen Skare
Mary Lou Bartz
David Peter Fedor

January

…wash me, and I shall be whiter than snow.
Psalm 51:7

For Him and Him Alone

"According to my earnest expectation and my hope,
that in nothing I shall be ashamed, but that with all
boldness, as always, so now also Christ shall be
magnified in my body, whether it be by life,
or by death."

PHILIPPIANS 1:20

Our love for Him is absolute and entire.
Nothing more does the Lord require.
Our utmost is for the Lord on high.
His will is our own, we will not deny.
We have stumbled and been discouraged.
From this day forth, we will be encouraged.
We will press on toward the goal and not turn back.
We know that in Christ, there is no lack.
He gives us courage; He has never faulted.
By life or by death, may Christ be exalted.

Lord, to You, we will commit our all.
We know You will help us; we will not fall.
When put to a test,
In Christ, we can rest.
This is our mission.
Act on God's commission.
God equips and makes us brave.
Praise the Lord! Our sins, He forgave.
If we meet with a crisis, we will not complain.
To live is Christ and to die is gain.

Do Not Depart in Ignorance

"By faith Abraham, when he was called
to go out into a place which he should
after receive for an inheritance, obeyed; and he went
out, not knowing whither he went."

HEBREWS 11:8

We know not where the Lord will lead.
We love Him and, to the Spirit, give heed.
We do not know what the Lord will do.
He reveals Himself to us; it is true.
Put each situation into God's hands.
He works things out; He understands.
Through many a conflict, we're put to a test.
We know He has promised; we will enter His rest.
In obedience, make no hesitation.
He leads the way to our destination.

Abraham went out, not knowing.
As he went, his faith kept growing.
We will go out, we know not why.
On His holy presence, we will rely.
Our God is all-wise;
Each day is a surprise.
He leads us out, one step at a time.
We have confident trust in the Lord, sublime.
Life has a purpose in this New Year.
God's holy presence, we do endear.

Obscurity and Absence of Light

"Clouds and darkness are round about Him;
righteousness and judgment are the
habitation of His throne."

PSALM 97:2

The Spirit within, reveals the true light.
Through clouds and darkness, He comes into sight.
The Holy Spirit interprets the Word.
He brings understanding to what we have heard.
We must realize who Jesus is.
We need first to become His.
There is great joy among the redeemed.
Things are much different than
what they have seemed.
The words that He speaks are spirit and life.
He meets us with truth in the midst of strife.

May His Word
Be heard.
Our God is Holy.
Trust Him wholly.
God's Word is alive.
By this, we survive.
Overcast skies and saddened hearts are obscure.
Be humble, repent, and receive Christ; be pure.
In the Word of God we take delight.
Worries and fears will then take flight.

Lord, What Will You Have Me to Do?

"Peter said unto Him, 'Lord, why cannot I follow thee
now? I will lay down my life for Thy sake.'"

JOHN 13:37

When there is doubt, continue to wait.
The Lord will direct; it is faith, not fate.
God will guide, don't run ahead.
He gives clear direction; by Him, be led.
Never barge ahead; be sure you are guided.
Be assured that, in God, you've confided.
Deny self and live your life for others.
Seek God first; reach out to sisters and brothers.
God has a master plan for our lives.
Don't stray from His path; His bidding survives.

When there is doubt,
Wait and don't go out.
Direct our steps, O Lord we pray.
Help us to walk in Your path today.
God's timing is always right.
Step by step, He sheds His light
May our selfish motives be restrained.
By the Lord, our steps are ordained.
When we walk with the Lord, we will not stumble.
Yielded hearts will obey and be humble.

The Spirit-Filled Life

"Simon Peter said unto Him, 'Lord, whither goest thou?' Jesus answered him, 'Whither I go, thou canst not follow Me now; but thou shalt follow Me afterwards.'"

JOHN 13:36

This is best; this is the way.
Just follow Jesus day by day.
The power to follow comes from within.
Build in this person; the victory, win.
To resolve to do better, we make a vow.
To rely on the Lord is the only how.
The Lord Jesus Christ is our firm foundation.
We must walk in the Spirit; He is our inspiration.
We want to follow Him this hour.
Trust in the Holy Spirit's power.

Let this be our recitation:
We will follow Jesus without hesitation.
Through the Spirit, our endower,
We need never fear or cower.
Oh Lord, for You, we hunger and thirst.
Love for God must always come first.
In order to do the Father's purposeful will,
Rely on the Spirit, our lives to fill.
In this hour, there is no greater need.
We must trust God to intervene as we plead.

Showing Reverence

"And he removed from thence unto a mountain on the
east of Bethel, and pitched his tent, having Bethel on
the west, and Hai on the east: and there he builded
an altar unto the LORD, and called upon the name of
the LORD."

GENESIS 12:8

Worship must be consistent
The call of the world is persistent.
Lord, You give the best; we give back in worship.
We praise and thank You and bask in Your fellowship.
Worship, wait and work in sweet communion.
To bless others, with God, there must be union.
God gives us gifts to give away.
The world awaits our help this day.
We constantly enjoy each blessing.
Give to others, in faith, confessing.

When we bask in God's presence,
The world sees His essence.
We must give the Lord our best.
The world awaits a harvest.
The Word, the walk, the worship---all three.
This is what He bestows upon you and me.
Praise the Lord! Await His orders and then go forth.
Go to the East, West, South and North.
Call upon the name of the Lord, everlasting.
Much good is performed through praying and fasting.

In Harmony with the Lord

"Jesus saith to him, 'Have I been so long time with you, and yet hast thou not known Me, Philip? He that hath seen Me hath seen the Father; and how sayest thou then, Show us the Father?'"

JOHN 14:9

To know the Lord is to bear good fruit.
Be one in thought, word and spirit; that's our pursuit.
In intimate friendship, He leads us on.
He is the One we can count upon.
Ask for anything in His name.
He did good works and still does the same.
Life in Jesus is our survival.
He will bring about revival.
To see Jesus is to see the Father
Jesus is the Way; all else is a bother.

Oh, how we long to know Him better.
Our every hang up, He will unfetter.
To carry out God's purpose, we must
constantly believe.
Keep yourself from evil and, to the Lord, cleave.
Now and throughout eternity,
We want to reach maturity.
We receive His blessings and know His Word.
We know Him and we have heard.
With Jesus we are closely related.
To do His will, we are consecrated.

Thoughts, Emotions and Feelings

"And they came to the place which God had told him
of; and Abraham built an altar there, and laid the
wood in order, and bound Isaac his son, and laid him
on the altar upon the wood."

GENESIS 22:9

Lord, make our lives a living sacrifice.
Only what is done through You will suffice.
Our lives have been sanctified and saved.
Only in Christ have we behaved.
God wants an offering that is living,
A surrendered life is one worth giving.
Jehovah-Jirah! The Lord will provide.
With all on the altar, in Him, we abide.
With Christ in control,
We are made whole.

In our humility,
God gives His ability.
We will give our lives in full surrender.
We need not fear; He is our defender.
When God's will is sincerely sought,
He enables us to do what we ought.
Jesus baptizes with the Holy Spirit and fire.
The Son has been glorified; it is He that we admire.
Over all creation, Christ is the firstborn.
He is the faithful, true witness; we need not be forlorn.

He's Alive!   I'm Alive!

"And the very God of peace sanctify you wholly; and I
pray God your whole spirit and soul and body be
preserved blameless unto the coming of our Lord
Jesus Christ."

1 THESSALONIANS 5:23

Search us, O God, and know our hearts.
Grace and mercy, our Lord imparts.
The Lord knows our thoughts before we speak it.
We want God's will; from the Lord, we seek it.
For His mercy, we have bidden.
From Him, nothing is hidden.
The blood of Jesus Christ cleanses us from all sin.
We're preserved blameless with His Spirit within.
God reaches deep and knows every thought.
The truth prevails when His will is sought.

Lord, be our guide
As, in You, we abide.
In Him we delight.
Walk in the Light.
Whenever there is a need,
Be sure to intercede.
God is with us in each situation.
We implore Him with great expectation.
From every form of evil, be sure to abstain.
False prophets may tempt us; in Christ we'll remain.

An Opportunity to be Enlightened

"To open their eyes, and to turn them from darkness
to light, and from the power of satan unto God, that
they may receive forgiveness of sins, and inheritance
among them which are sanctified by
faith that is in Me."

ACTS 26:18

Natural man, sins have committed.
Through the cross, those sins are remitted.
Open our eyes that we may see.
Great things God does guarantee.
When born-again we began to understand.
He is our Friend; He holds our hand.
To turn from darkness to light is to be converted.
From sinful ways, we've been diverted.
From our sins, we have received remission.
We preach the gospel; that is our commission.

To be obedient
Is expedient.
Our hearts are cleansed; the gift is received.
Go forth; make disciples of those who have believed.
When belief is our plight,
We receive our sight.
May our minds be opened to the truth.
The Word of God will calm and sooth.
Be stiff-necked no longer; in the Lord delight.
Fear the Lord and do His works; His way is right.

His Commission and Our Submission

"And as they led Him away, they laid hold upon one
Simon, a Cyrenian, coming out of the country, and on
him they laid the cross, that he
might bear it after Jesus."

LUKE 23:26

Our obedience to God may, to some people, offend.
The message of the cross we must defend.
Just follow Him; He will take care of the rest.
Trust and obey; He knows what is best.
Circumstances may cause misery and pain.
True to the Lord, we will remain.
Christians, united, serve the Lord with a common aim.
Great things are accomplished in Jesus' name.
When we love the Lord we want to do right.
It is in Him that we delight.

When we obey the Lord, we do what is needed.
We will love Him; to His will we have heeded.
We will not suffer loss.
We must adhere to the cross.
Our obedience may come at a cost.
We reject selfish plans to save the lost.
We will not be contrary.
The cross, we will carry.
Crowds may protest, rant and rave.
Remember this: Christ came to save.

Closet Prayer

"But without a parable spake He not unto them: and
when they were alone, He expounded all
things to His disciples."

MARK 4:34

When alone with God, He will encourage.
Self-will and pride only discourage.
We sometimes begin to murmur and complain.
Talk to God; He will comfort and sustain.
God reveals our foolish pride.
Our thoughts and feelings we cannot hide.
When proud of ourselves, we are
somewhat conceited.
God directs, so let us not be defeated.
Many are lost and want to know.
Proclaim the Gospel; plant seed and watch it grow.

Be alone with God; be still.
With love, your cup He will fill.
God will inform.
We will conform.
What a special place in the secret closet.
Our pride and self-worth we deposit.
Meet Him daily in the secret place.
Our cares and worries He will erase.
Find a quiet corner; He is always there.
He is waiting, His nature to share.

In His Sanctuary – A Secret Meeting

"And when He was alone, they that were about Him
with the twelve asked of Him the parable."

MARK 4:10

God's truth, will He expound.
We will find that we are heaven bound.
Christ gives love, grace and His abiding presence.
He deals in truth and not in nonsense.
Hard times bring us to our knees.
To God, our Father, we make our pleas.
To be taught of the Lord is to know what is true.
The message of the kingdom, He will reveal to you.
Great words of wisdom to us are shown.
We love to meet with our Lord alone.

We are with Jesus while in a crowd,
His speech is silent; His inner voice is loud.
Of private prayer,
Be well aware.
The Counselor will teach us all things.
Holiness is what He brings.
When God's perfect will we seek,
He alone is who will speak.
Parables revealed the kingdom's mystery.
The lessons proclaimed will speak throughout history.

Compelled to Serve the Lord

"Also I heard the voice of the Lord, saying, 'Whom
shall I send, and who will go for us?' Then said I,
'Here am I; send me.'"

ISAIAH 6:8

God's plea goes out to everyone.
The message is: Accept the Son.
Those who follow, He will send.
The summons of God, He does extend.
There is no exemption from God's call.
His request goes out to one and all.
The chosen ones are, to God, related.
We are His children and we are dedicated.
We hear God's appointments when in His presence.
He wants us to follow Him with great persistence.

Yes, God's urgent claim goes out.
Please comprehend.
Hear His voice: "Whom shall I send?"
Lord, keep us from falling.
Help us to listen to Your calling.
Here we are; send us, we say.
We will do God's will today.
God sends a message and makes a plea.
We are here for His purpose; go forth in victory.
The call of God goes out; we are willing to hear.
Be still and know; His Word is sincere.

Complete Consecration

"Therefore we are buried with him by baptism into
death: that like as Christ was raised up from the dead
by the glory of the Father, even so we also should
walk in newness of life."

ROMANS 6:4

For the Lord, we are set apart and made new.
We love Him with all our hearts; that is true.
A sanctified life has only one goal.
Let the Lord have full control.
We want to have spiritual fitness.
Die to self and, of Him, be a witness.
No longer need we sin, as a slave.
With a new life in Christ we will behave.
When raised with Him, He gives newness of life.
We walk in His light; He frees us from strife.

True believers are born anew.
The life of Christ will faith renew.
To self, we are dead.
We live in Christ, instead.
We are justified and sanctified.
May this be testified.
We are no longer worried.
In Christ, we are buried.
We walk in newness of life; may the Lord be praised.
We walk in the Spirit,
because Jesus Christ was raised.

Listen to His Still, Small Voice

"I heard the voice of the Lord saying,
'Whom shall I send, and who will go for us?'
Then said I, 'Here am I; send me.'"

ISAIAH 6:8

God welcomes us; we are related.
His will, not ours, is firmly stated.
When hearts are changed, we hear God's call.
His message is profound to all.
To the voice of God, we will be attuned.
With our Savior, we have communed.
We desire to be spiritually mature.
We need to put on God's holy nature.
Many are waiting to hear the Good News.
We will willingly go; His way we will choose.

His disposition within can be achieved.
The Holy Spirit we have received.
The whole world, for salvation, is needy.
May we share the Word and not be greedy.
The Lord wants to send us.
We will join and sing the heavenly chorus.
Each moment is an opportunity, Christ to reveal.
His Presence and Power have radiant appeal.
Our commission from God is to go and tell.
He leads and guides us; the Word does compel.

Make God's Nature Your I.D.

"But when it pleased God, who separated me from my
mother's womb, and called me by His grace, to reveal
His Son in me, that I might preach Him among the
heathen; immediately I conferred not with
flesh and blood:"

GALATIANS 1:15-16

The Lord, to us, has been revealed.
We love Him and reach others; He has appealed.
The life of Christ is our desire.
In His employment, He will hire.
God's divine nature we do observe.
He causes us to love and serve.
He called us with His favor and blessing.
Now, His Name we are confessing.
Jesus, God the Son, has been revealed.
We'll proclaim His glory and, to the Spirit, yield.

Unto God the Father, we have kneeled.
His abiding presence has appealed.
Be generous
With Jesus.
We hear God's urgent call.
Jesus is pleading for us all.
May this one thing be resolved.
Don't just say and observe; in Christ, be involved.
Day by day, we sometimes are taken up in busyness.
God wants us to know we should
be doing His business.

The Perfect Supreme Being

"And Thomas answered and said unto Him, 'My Lord
and my God.'"

JOHN 20:28

Give whatever you don't use.
As you witness, you won't lose.
Bless the Lord, Oh my soul.
As we praise, You take control.
From devotion to Jesus, do not swerve.
Love Him first and foremost; then serve.
To the Lord Jesus Christ be loyal.
Crown Him King in your heart, most royal.
Doubt and refusal will bring disaster.
In reality, we call Him Master.

Give God pleasure.
He is our treasure.
When, to God, we are devoted,
True love will be promoted.
We owe to Christ our first allegiance.
It is reflected in our obedience.
What a blessed privilege to be part of His plan.
He became incarnate to reach down to man.
No longer are we giving heed to sinful vices.
We are devoted to God and are living sacrifices.

To See or Not to See

"And when the sun was going down, a deep sleep fell upon Abram; and, lo, an horror of great darkness fell upon him."

GENESIS 15:12

Thoughts, upon the Lord, are stayed.
He will answer; I have prayed.
God's vision is bright, but the world is dark.
Keep your eyes on the Lord; don't miss the mark.
Be still and listen; hear Him speak.
Put God first; it is Him we seek.
With our eyes on the Lord, He gives the vision.
It is then, He sends us on our mission.
Attune your ears to God's good advice.
With His truth, He will energize.

Wait upon God; in Him be grounded.
Be a part of the Church that He has founded.
From darkness to dawn,
We must carry on.
We will listen and be still.
Learn to do the Father's will.
Upon the Lord, our minds will stay.
We will trust Him to light our way.
The wise will shine; they have been transformed.
By His presence and guidance,
we have been informed.

Embrace New Life, in Christ

"Jesus answered and said unto him, 'Verily, verily, I say unto thee, Except a man be born again, he cannot see the kingdom of God.'"

JOHN 3:3

Day by day, God leads the way.
Fresh thoughts renew in a grand array.
Obedience to the Lord is fresh, not stale.
His message of love will not fail.
Do not grow weary and tired,
Be freshly renewed and inspired.
When we walk in the flesh our words are mundane.
Fresh word from the Spirit will not be spoken in vain.
New birth in Christ is necessary.
Of any other way to salvation, be wary.

We need not search for things to do.
The Spirit leads and, with life, will make new.
When the well seems dry,
He will refresh and supply
New life in Christ, we will embrace.
He will help us each day to face.
Very often, new opportunities are presented.
We have no reason to be bored and discontented.
There is no end to the supplies God gives.
In fullness of joy, the true believer lives.

Remember What God Bears in Mind

"Go and cry in the ears of Jerusalem, saying, 'Thus saith the LORD; 'I remember thee, the kindness of thy youth, the love of thine espousals, when thou wentest after Me in the wilderness, in a land that was not sown.'"

JEREMIAH 2:2

Each thought and deed is a reflection.
God is love; in Him is perfection.
We are responsible for God's reputation.
Rejoice in Him with exultation.
Let us return to the love we first had.
When we were set free our hearts were glad.
Trust in the Lord with deep devotion.
May the desire to please Him be your emotion.
Fearlessly announce the given message.
Fools deny the prophetic passage.

Always remember what God treasures.
He, alone, gives abundant pleasures.
There is no need to be sad,
We, in Christ, are in righteousness clad.
With the goal in mind, we win the prize.
To live in obedience is always wise.
Let not our thoughts and actions be put to shame.
To fill God's heart with gladness will be our aim.
Our love, first for God, we must constantly nourish.
Feast on the Word of God, our new life will flourish.

Away From Circumstances, Up to God

"Look unto Me, and be ye saved, all the ends of the
earth: for I am God, and there is none else."

ISAIAH 45:22

So often, we take blessings for granted.
When troubles come, in Christ be planted.
In our trials, we draw closer to Him.
He comes to save; be no longer grim.
It is written in the Holy Book.
Accept salvation; to Jesus look.
God desires that all people be converted.
Each individual should be alerted.
The Lord desires that all be changed.
Look to Jesus; in Him, life is rearranged.

The Lord supplies our daily bread.
By His Word, each one is fed.
As we trust in the Lord.
We receive our reward.
God desires conversion of all.
Trust in Him and you will not fall.
When bogged down with troubles, trials, and scurry,
Put your trust in Jesus; in Him, you won't worry.
When all around us there seems to be unrest,
Remember, our hope is in Jesus; we are blessed.

A Change by Power of Discernment

"But we all, with open face beholding as in a glass the glory of the Lord, are changed into the same image from glory to glory, even as by the Spirit of the Lord."

11 CORINTHIANS 3:18

Search us, oh God, and show us our faults,
Until our lives, Your spirit exalts.
Look to the Lord and behold His splendor.
He is our Savior and our defender.
We behold His glory as in a glass.
The mirror reflects whatever He has.
On God's triumph the believer reflects.
To become like Him is what He expects.
Through the Spirit, we are transformed.
In us, the life of Christ is formed.

On the Lord, we set our affection.
Stand back, and get the right reflection.
It is God that we behold.
He changes lives and makes us bold.
Learn
And discern.
Behold the glory in godly meditations.
We have set upon the Lord, our adorations.
Into the mirror of our heart, mind, and soul we look.
To be filled with Jesus, we must read the Holy Book.

Which Way? God's Way!

"But rise, and stand upon thy feet: for I have appeared unto thee for this purpose, to make thee a minister and a witness both of these things which thou hast seen, and of those things in which I will appear unto thee;"

ACTS 26:16

The only choice that will please us,
Is to surrender our lives to Jesus.
The Lord now sends us on a mission.
Bear fruit in Him; that is our vision.
God's purpose for us can be attained.
When led by the Spirit, we are retrained.
To the Lord Jesus Christ, we are devoted.
He, alone, is to be promoted.
Prove your repentance by your deeds.
The Lord supplies us in our needs.

My life, to the Lord, is dedicated.
To do His will, I'm obligated.
God gives meaning to our lives.
When yielded to Him, our spirit revives.
Listen and pray.
He shows us the way.
God's intention overpowers.
Jesus only fills our hours.
Jesus came for us, our sins to atone.
Our purpose in life is for Him alone.

He is Right There, to Share Your Care

"For God, who commanded the light to shine out of
darkness, hath shined in our hearts, to give the light
of the knowledge of the glory of God in the face of
Jesus Christ."

II CORINTHIANS 4:6

In God's good pleasure, He comes on the scene.
He fills us with wonder and keeps our hearts clean.
Expectancy is the key to blessing.
He is Lord. We are confessing.
With God, for God, and in God; we are set apart.
Have faith and believe with all your heart.
He has called us by His grace.
His presence we embrace.
It is God's good pleasure that He come into view.
He is right there, our thoughts to renew.

Make room for the Spirit to move.
When we do, our lives will improve.
Prepare and present; expect God to act.
We depend upon the Spirit, in fact.
With great anticipation,
Expect God's participation.
Our order of service is typed and presented.
The move of the Spirit should not be resented.
Look up and expect; God gives joy and not gloom.
He has a message to bring; prepare Him room.

Consider Him and Be Set Apart

"Wherefore, if God so clothe the grass of the field,
which today is, and tomorrow is cast into the oven,
shall He not much more clothe you,
O ye of little faith?"

MATTHEW 6:30

Our lives, to God, are consecrated.
From evil, He is separated.
God clothes the lilies of the field.
Be not anxious; to Him yield.
Receive His Spirit; on Him rely.
He will give; He will not deny.
The Heavenly Father will give much more.
Our cup is much fuller than before.
A seed that is planted will sprout and life show.
May your roots grow deep, and good fruit grow.

For the Lord, we thirst.
We will put Him first.
Begin anew each day.
Trust Him as you pray.
On the Word, concentrate.
To the Lord, consecrate.
For sacred use, we are set apart.
Trust in the Lord with all your heart.
Listen to the Word of God and, with it, cooperate.
Our hearts are in tune; with God, we communicate.

God's Will is Number One

"Therefore I say unto you, 'Take no thought for your life, what ye shall eat, or what ye shall drink; nor yet for your body, what ye shall put on. Is not the life more than meat, and the body then raiment?'"

MATTHEW 6:25

Be not overly concerned about lack.
Look to the Lord; He's coming back!
The Spirit of God raises up a standard.
To trust in our riches, we give no regard.
Take no thought what the world's future holds.
Moment by moment, your life unfolds.
Our relationship with God is what matters.
When Christians unite, the enemy scatters.
Don't worry; in Christ, we will not be poor.
We meet each day and He gives much more.

There is no need to rush and hurry.
Trust in the Lord, and do not worry.
This world's riches do not satisfy.
Of riches in Christ Jesus, we will testify.
Put your trust in the Son.
He is always number one.
If we yearn for riches, we get bogged down with care.
Seek the kingdom of God and the gospel share.
Life is more important than food and clothes.
Our needs are supplied; our Provider knows.

No Merit to Disappoint Our Lord

"And when we were all fallen to the earth, I heard a voice speaking un to me, and saying in the Hebrew tongue, 'Saul, Saul, why persecutest thou Me? It is hard for thee to kick against the pricks.'"

ACTS 26:14

In going our own way, we are obstinate.
In Christ, we will be compassionate.
We must not insist upon our own way.
Self-will, be gone! The Lord, obey.
To our convictions, we will be firm.
To God's word, we will affirm.
Prove your repentance by your deeds.
Through saving faith, God meets our needs.
Be alive with the Holy Spirit's fire.
Make the Lord your one desire.

Abandon selfish pleasures.
Accept God's treasures.
In Christ we are sanctified.
The Word of truth is not denied.
Jesus was unjustly oppressed.
In disobedience, we are distressed.
True repentance is proved by our deeds.
We are saved by faith in Christ and the Spirit leads.
Faith is victorious; our Lord is always just.
To proclaim God's Word is what He does entrust.

No Merit To Be Absolutely Uninformed

"And I said, 'Who art thou, Lord?'
And He said, 'I am Jesus whom thou persecutest.'"

ACTS 26:15

God is in our circumstances.
Each holy event, the Lord enhances.
God does not give us uncertain paces.
His love prevails in preordained places.
Oh, our God, we delight to do Your will.
We will obey Your voice and You will fulfill.
We have a longing to do what the Lord desires.
We will read the Word and He inspires.
We don't do just what we want to do.
To His direction we will be faithful and true.

His way is our way.
We trust Him each day.
In our hearts, He is on the throne.
We belong to Him; we are His own.
Believers call Him Lord.
Faith is His sincere reward.
To do God's will is our affection.
The Holy Spirit will give us direction.
With all our hearts, it is Him we seek.
He is Lord; of His love, we will speak.

A Confrontation with Willingness to Obey

"And Samuel lay until the morning,
and opened the doors of the house of the LORD.
And Samuel feared to show Eli the vision."

I SAMUEL 3:15

He calls us and He does the work.
Yield to Him and do not shirk.
The great I AM meets every need.
He has said so; to Him give heed.
Don't trust the advice of fellow man.
It may be the opposite of God's plan.
What did God say? This we inquire.
Walk not in the flesh; may the Spirit inspire.
The God of peace will sanctify.
The Word He gives, do not deny.

Only God can make holy and whole.
We are put together in body, spirit and soul.
Here I am; send me;
I will go; I am free.
With a life of obedience,
We walk forth with competence.
God gives His royal permission.
He sends us out upon His mission.
The Lord walks with us throughout each day.
Help us, Lord, your instruction to obey.

Reality is Redemption

"Paul, a servant of Jesus Christ, called to be an
apostle, separated unto the Gospel of God,"

ROMANS 1:1

We are delivered from sin; we are saved.
We are no longer, by the enemy, enslaved.
Let the redeemed proclaim the Good News.
Christ is reality; Him, we will choose.
We will be enthused and fervent,
We are called by Him to be His servant.
As special messengers, we are set apart to preach.
Good News is the message;
our loving Lord will teach.
The Gospel of God is committed to our trust.
He enables; the ministry is a must.

When Jesus we know,
Our faith will grow.
Without the Lord, my life is nil.
Oh, Holy Spirit, come and fill.
The Gospel is God's power.
Lord, rain down a heavenly shower
The Word of God is what we preach.
Salvation is the message; souls we will reach.
The din of the world is badly corrupted.
May salvation be preached and the din interrupted.

February

For God so loved the world, that He gave his only begotten Son, that whosoever believeth in Him should not perish, but have everlasting life. John 3:16

Lift up Jesus

"For Christ sent me not to baptize, but to preach the
Gospel: not with wisdom of words, lest the cross of
Christ should be made of none effect."

I CORINTHIANS 1:17

God's call is to preach the message affirmed.
May the testimony of Christ be, in you, confirmed.
When we tell of His love, to Him, they'll be drawn.
Redemption is through Him, our sin is gone.
Jesus calls us to be His friend.
Our romance with the world must end.
To preach the Gospel is our fashion.
Upon the world, God has compassion.
We need not be of eloquent speech.
The glad tidings of redemption, we will teach.

Preach the truth, without exemption.
Reality is redemption.
Amazing Grace will be our song,
Yes, to the Lord, we do belong.
The Lord, alone, is great.
We pray and, on Him, wait.
Through heartbreak and trouble, faith does develop.
When times are hard, we must lift Him up.
Listen to the Savior's call.
On the cross, He died for all.

The Compelling Force of the Summons

"For though I preach the gospel, I have nothing to glory of: for necessity is laid upon me; yea, woe is unto me, if I preach not the Gospel!"

1 CORINTHIANS 9:16

Come to Him and He will save.
No more let sins enslave.
We are saved is what we testify.
Our greatest need, He does supply.
Unto the Lord, we are set apart.
We will love Him with all our heart.
Lethargy makes us filled with woe.
With glad tidings, we must go.
Neglecting the salvation message
is no reason to boast.
Jesus is Lord; He must be foremost.

Be a co-worker.
Be not a shirker.
We love the Lord; with Him we are one.
Tell the Good News; lift up Jesus, the Son.
Witnesses we shall be.
Tell others of Jesus and you will see.
The call of the world with God's call competes.
As we walk with the Lord, selfish ways He defeats.
Look not back; look to God for correction.
The Lord will lead us; He gives us direction.

The Proclamation of Kindred Spirits

"Being defamed, we intreat: we are made as the filth of the world, and are the off scouring of all things unto this day."

I CORINTHIANS 4:13

Christ was smitten and despised.
In Him, our faith is exercised.
Our own righteousness is as filthy rags.
The chicken-hearted boasts and brags.
Disciples have many trials to endure.
Through them all, He keeps us pure.
Following Christ may mean suffering and pain.
Safe in His love we choose to remain.
In Christ's suffering, we have our share.
Peace is our rule; it is brought by prayer.

Do not, by the world, be defiled.
May the voice of evil be reviled.
We love the Lord; in Him we grow.
Our lives are transformed; this we know.
Sinful ways, we will defy.
We are born-again and will testify.
The world may meet us with contempt.
Our reverence for God will make despair exempt.
A servant of Christ has inward peace.
Our goal is to share and blessings release.

Individual Motivational Force

"For the love of Christ constraineth us; because we
thus judge, that if one died for all, then were all dead:
And that He died for all, that they which live should
not henceforth live unto themselves, but unto Him
which died for them, and rose again."

11 CORINTHIANS 5:14-15

God's love holds us in His power.
He, alone, is the great endower.
What wondrous things the Lord has done,
Through the overwhelming love of Christ, the Son.
By the love of Christ we are compelled.
We die to self, His life excelled.
We are in His embrace; we are held fast.
We need not dwell on sins of the past.
We are constrained and no longer proud.
Only God's grace is what is allowed.

The Spirit moves; He does set free.
A life in Christ brings victory.
By the love of Christ, sin He has repelled.
Worldly standards should be expelled.
We are witnesses to who He is.
Self-glory, He will dismiss.
We will adhere to our Christian belief.
We stand firm in faith; God is our Chief.
We are messengers of Jesus, and His Mighty Power.
The world needs this proclamation in this hour.

Do You Put It Off, Or Do It Now?

"Yea, and if I be offered upon the sacrifice and service
of your faith, I joy, and rejoice with you all."

PHILIPPIANS 2:17

Lord, take our lives and set us free.
They are an offering of love to Thee.
When God chooses our work, we will obey.
We will joy and rejoice with love to convey.
Salvation is a free gift that we cannot earn.
Through good example, others will learn.
Lord, make our lives a living sacrifice.
Rid us of selfish sin and vice.
This is no time to be depressed and pout.
Like a drink offering, our lives are poured out.

When, of Christianity, we taste,
Our lives are full and not lives of waste.
Earthly treasures fade and die.
Life in Christ does satisfy.
We will be a blessing poured.
We walk closely with the Lord.
Lord, our lives to You we present.
We will rejoice; in Christ we are content.
By what is a true follower of Christ implied?
A humble servant is not necessarily dignified.

Meet the Crisis with New Boldness

"For I am now ready to be offered, and the time of my
departure is at hand."

11 TIMOTHY 4:6

All our lives, to Him, we give.
In His appointed will, we will live.
Lord, we are ready to be offered.
We are willing; Your way is proffered.
We are made pure as if through fire.
In the midst of crisis, He's our desire.
The Lord wills that we put our all on the altar.
From His divine plan, we will not falter.
We eagerly long for Christ's return.
He will rule and reign; for this we yearn.

The Spirit moves; He does set free.
A life in Christ brings victory.
Dejection discourages.
Faith encourages.
Our offering is life.
God will help us face the strife.
Lord, help us to be ready for whatever You send.
We know not when our earth's journey will end.
On the altar, the sacrifice is bound.
After sincere repentance, new hope is found.

Improved Behavior Through Put Downs

"And how the chief priests and our rulers delivered
Him to be condemned to death, and have crucified
Him. But we trusted that it had been He which should
have redeemed Israel: and beside all this, today is
the third day since these things were done."

LUKE 24:20, 21

We should never be depressed.
With the love of God, we are impressed.
Seek not the gift, but seek the giver.
Keep on trusting; He does deliver.
We must not insist on our own way.
Dejection fills us with dismay.
Depression and oppression is the enemy's plea.
When he tells us to be sad, we will disagree.
God is with us in our simple tasks.
He willingly supplies what the believer asks.

Fire produces the finest gold.
May this, of our lives, be told.
God answers prayer in His time.
The results will be sublime.
According to God's will, we have been sent for.
We must do what we are meant for.
Mercy and love are what we all savor.
Once deliverance comes, we live in God's favor.
No longer need we, with the world, compete.
God works in our hearts; in Christ, we are complete.

This Moment Set Me Apart Completely

"Faithful is He that calleth you, who also will do it."

1 THESSALONIANS 5: 24

Worldly pleasures, we can deny.
Be sanctified wholly is our reply.
When fully yielded unto the Master,
He will keep us from disaster.
May God sanctify you through and through.
He is faithful that called you and also will do.
Oh Lord, we want to do Your will alone.
It is only then that Your likeness will be shone.
We must be willing to do our part.
This goal is reached when Christ rules the heart.

In Christ Jesus we abide,
For His glory, we are set aside.
Lord, we want to know You.
Lord, we want to grow in You.
Lord, what is Your point of view?
Sanctify us and make us new.
Our thoughts of God must be intense.
Our hearts are sincere; there is no pretense.
Our Lord spoke in parables;
the disciples understood.
Many lessons He did teach;
He told them what is good.
We must stay awake and await His return.
He is coming again; for this we yearn.

Is Fatigue Your League?

"Hast thou not known? hast thou not heard, that the everlasting God, the LORD, the Creator of the ends of the earth, fainteth not, neither is weary? there is no searching of His understanding."

ISAIAH 40:28

Feed on the Word that you may feed others.
Tell friends and neighbors, sisters and brothers.
New Christians must be nourished.
Feed them the Word till they have flourished.
The Lord is the everlasting God, the Creator.
He rules and reigns; there is none greater.
The Lord does not get tired or weary.
He enables us to cheer up the dreary.
Trust in the Lord; He is the source.
He will keep our lives on course.

Feed the flock that they be healthy.
The flock will then be spiritually wealthy.
The Good Shepherd, a watch does keep.
We will do our best to feed the sheep.
We will not be deprived of strength and vitality.
May our personal quality be Christ's personality.
There is a continuous supply of living water to drink.
As channels of blessing; we have more than we think.
God sends us help according to our need.
He has love and forgiveness; to the Spirit, give heed.

Look Ever to Jesus!

"Lift up your eyes on high, and behold who hath created these things, that bringeth out their host by number: He calleth them all by names by the greatness of His might, for that He is strong in power; not one faileth."

ISAIAH 40:26

Man-made idols obstruct our view.
Trust fully in God and faith renew.
Our eyes must be focused on the Creator.
He, alone, is our emancipator.
God deserves our worship and praise.
The Name of Jesus we will raise.
Think on what God, our Lord, has created.
When we look upon nature, our hearts are elated.
Look up toward heaven and behold.
His power and strength are worth more than gold.

Be careful what you look upon.
This world's false gods must be gone.
From earthly treasures turn away.
Focus on the Lord each day
Carnal ways blind our eyes.
Look to Jesus and be wise.
Look up and see that God is good.
On Him we depend for our livelihood.
Of possessions and accomplishments,
we will not boast.
The harvest of souls for the kingdom matters most.

The Father's Enduring Love

Is Your Expectation Alive and Well?

"Thou wilt keep him in perfect peace, whose mind is
stayed on Thee: because he trusteth in Thee. Trust
ye in the LORD forever: for in the LORD JEHOVAH
is everlasting strength:

ISAIAH 26:3-4

How awesome everything we find,
When God is centermost in mind.
God is mightier than any imagination.
He holds us in awesome fascination.
Christ, our Rock, is a sure and firm foundation.
He brings peace and rest to each generation.
He's a stable ground on which we can stand.
He is steadfast and faithful; heed His command.
Our minds and purpose, on the Lord, will stay.
His peace is ours; it will not go away.

Look! The harvest field is ready.
Go forth to reap with a faith that is steady.
Our minds upon the Lord are stayed.
We trust in Him and we have prayed.
This one thing we must realize.
Don't lose your power to visualize.
New every day are the blessings God bestows.
As we feast on the Word,
faith is nourished and grows.
We hear and are obedient to the voice that He raises.
With music and song, we extol Him with praises.

Advice? Must I Listen?

"And Moses said unto the people, 'Fear not: for God is come to prove you, and that His fear may be before your faces, that ye sin not.'"

EXODUS 20:20

O Lord, we want to hear Your voice.
To do Your will, will be our choice.
To study His Word is a great need.
He commands and we will take heed.
Love the Lord and walk on His path.
The humble, He will save from wrath.
When we refuse to hear, we are put to shame.
Much can be accomplished in Jesus' name.
Speak Lord, and we will listen.
Behold, Your bright light will glisten.

We are compelled to read the Word.
It is there that God's voice is heard.
Read the Word and obey His commands.
All else may fail; the Word of God stands.
Go first to the source.
That is the Scripture, of course.
Through our lives, may God's glory shine.
The truth must prevail, the saints to refine.
We can cry out to God, in Jesus' name,
with assurance.
His love, care, and goodness gives endurance.

Consecrated, Intuitive Judgment

"And the LORD came, and stood, and called as at
other times, 'Samuel, Samuel.' Then Samuel
answered, 'Speak; for thy servant heareth.'"

1 SAMUEL 3:10

We know, Lord, you always hear us.
You are omnipresent; yes, always near us.
God speaks to us in many ways.
His love and mercy He displays.
Speak Lord; we want to hear what You say.
Your revelation, we can hear every day.
We rest assured, that God hears our prayer.
He is present everywhere.
Sometimes we may fret and agonize.
God is speaking; His voice we recognize.

We will hear, respond, and our love commit.
As He speaks, we will submit.
God's voice is present in the Word.
The servant listens; he has heard.
A faithful servant,
Must listen and be fervent.
The world makes noises to distract.
To the Christian, the truth does attract.
God wants us to have peace and to be still.
We shall hear and respond, as we do His will.

Training the Mind to be Attentive

"What I tell you in darkness, that speak ye in light:
and what ye hear in the ear, that preach
ye upon the housetops."

MATTHEW 10:27

While feeling somber, we will listen and give heed.
There God meets us in our need.
He turns obscurity into light.
He tells us how to make things right.
No one is exempt from gloomy days.
What God tells you will amaze.
To the Word of God and its truth remain.
Be not afraid; God will sustain.
When troubles come, don't complain and mumble.
Trials work to make us humble.

Read and meditate upon the Word; God will teach.
The light will shine when the truth you preach.
Tell not the tales of sadness.
When healing appears, there is gladness.
In troublesome times, be not retentive.
To the Lord, be attentive.
Humility occurs and our hearts soften.
In dire circumstances, our prayers are often.
The message God speaks in the dark
is of great price.
We share what we have learned;
we'll give good advice.

Accountable for the Other's Faith?

"For none of us liveth to himself and no
man dieth to himself."

ROMANS 14:7

Be dead to self and alive to Christ.
Remember how He sacrificed.
We have a desire to be efficient.
God, alone, will be sufficient.
God gives us what we should share.
He spreads His blessings everywhere.
Be broken bread and poured out wine.
God always gives us what is just fine.
Whether we live or die, to the Lord we belong.
We're called to be witnesses; He is our song.

To help each other, we're assigned.
Love the Lord and all humankind.
We have a flock to keep.
Jesus tells us to feed His sheep.
May we not be put upon the shelf.
Let Jesus shine and not self.
Know the Lord; love Him and serve Him well.
Seize the privilege, the Gospel to tell.
Supply what is needed to other believers.
Many are waiting to be faith-building receivers.

Wake Up From Your Deep Slumber

"Wherefore He saith, 'Awake thou that sleepest, and arise from the dead, and Christ shall give thee light.'"

EPHESIANS 5:14

Awake, my soul, arise and shine.
I'm captured by His love divine.
We know this to be a fact:
The Holy Spirit inspires us to act.
We must move ahead, when we are inspired.
Action, on our part, is required.
Light makes all things visible.
Let us do only what is permissible.
Jesus asks us to stretch forth our hand.
He, alone, will help us stand.

Get up and get going.
Let your faith be showing.
It's time to move.
Fears remove.
When our thoughts are inspired,
Faithful action is required.
Our command is to move ahead.
Take the first step and go forth as you are led.
When we overcome, God gives us the ability.
As we trust and obey, He gives us stability.

Don't Deny the Truth of Your Joy

"And as he lay and slept under a juniper tree, behold, then an angel touched him, and said unto him, 'Arise and eat.'"

I KINGS 19:5

Repress depression
Exalt with expression.
There is blackness; flee from it.
Move ahead in the Spirit.
When disappointed, rise up and eat.
Meet depression with defeat.
Live on a higher plane of life today.
Don't worry or fret; get up and obey.
Don't wallow in your sadness.
Look to the Lord; be filled with gladness.

What is that in your hand?
Use it for what God has planned.
Are you impressed?
It should be expressed.
We will not pout and be sad.
In the Lord, we are glad.
Don't live a life of defeat.
The Bread of Life is what we eat.
Pursue that which will encourage and bless.
Be a channel of blessing; God's love possess.

Give God Your Heavy Cares

"Rise, let us be going: behold, he is at hand that doth
betray Me."

MATTHEW 26:46

The past is forgiven; we need not fret.
In Him, we are living; our needs are met.
Has an opportunity been lost?
Move ahead at any cost.
Leave past behind; do not despair.
Put the future in God's care.
We must move ahead; God does insist.
His plan for us we will not resist.
Fear and dismay are unhealthy distractions.
Arise and shine; put yourself into actions.

Take charge; don't be despondent.
Be a good news correspondent.
Awake and be going.
Your faith is growing.
The past, we will forget.
Don't live in regret.
Look not back on what is undone.
March ever onward; a new day is begun.
The Lord does not want us to be downhearted.
New opportunities and abundant life is imparted.

The First Step Against Monotony

"ARISE, shine; for thy light is come, and the glory of
the LORD is risen upon thee."

ISAIAH 60:1

When we awaken, He is there.
The Lord, our Lord is everywhere.
The task set before us may look hard.
What God perfects is no longer marred.
Step out in faith; Arise and shine!
The drudgery becomes divine.
Jesus set for us an example.
Do as He did; that will be ample.
The Lord loves the world to the highest degree.
He shed His blood for you and for me.

First pray; and then, get up and go.
As you obey, your pledged word will grow.
In faith, we will step out.
Don't just sit and pout.
When we walk with the Lord,
We will never be bored.
Many essential duties are performed each day.
May the light of Jesus shine in what we do and say.
Each day is a new opportunity.
Yesterday is gone; advance in Christian unity.

Unrealistic Fancies

"But that the world may know that I love the Father;
and as the Father gave Me commandment, even so I
do. Arise, let us go hence."

JOHN 14:31

Life is not just a dream.
It is the Lord that we esteem.
Let us get up and go:
The love of God will show.
Be still and then, obey.
His Word will light the way.
Don't just sit or stand, but go!
The Lord supplies the overflow.
Come now, let us leave.
What God has promised, we receive.

See the vision.
Go forth with His mission.
Don't be discouraged.
Be taught and encouraged.
Trust Him every day.
Go out and obey.
God sets the course.
He does not use force.
The inspiration is given for a reason.
Remember, it is now the harvest season.

Am I of Any Use or Value to God?

"And Jesus said, 'Let her alone; why trouble ye her?
She hath wrought a good work on Me.'"

MARK 14:6

To Your Spirit, we will yield,
In You, we have been sealed.
It's the little things that count.
With perfect love, He does surmount.
God is in each ordinary task.
He does far more than what we ask.
Simple obedience is our greatest need,
To His direction, always give heed.
What God does through us is worthy of praise.
His accomplishments are sure to amaze.

To love is to commit.
Wholesome deeds we will submit.
Love God sincerely.
Embrace Him dearly.
How can we, to others, the Lord attract?
Trust each spontaneous, loving act.
From God and for His glory, take no vacation.
The Lord is not a hobby or an avocation.
When, to God, our lives are fully yielded,
From the enemy's darts we are shielded.

Hold Fast and Stand Firm

"Be still, and know that I am God: I will be exalted
among the heathen, I will be exalted in the earth."

PSALM 46:10

We know the Lord is on the throne.
He reigns supreme; we are not alone.
We know we are on the winning side,
When, in Christ, we do abide.
Tenacity is more than endurance.
We must trust with great assurance.
The great I AM will be exalted.
Sin and darkness, He has halted.
Give to God the proper place.
He helps us to win the race.

Oh Lord, make us pure.
Through every hardship, we may endure.
In the midst of stress,
Worship, praise, and confess.
With discipline, we persevere.
Be still and know; God's Word, revere.
When we have His assurance,
We can march on with endurance.
In His leading, be confident.
When we trust in God, faith is evident.

Resolved to Minister the Love of God

"Even as the Son of man came not to be ministered
unto, but to minister, and to give His life
a ransom for many."

MATTHEW 20:28

To all, we will bring the truth.
It is needed by the old, middle-aged and youth.
What's most important is to love the Lord.
When we do that, the Word is our sword.
Love for Jesus is our aim.
We strive not for our own glory or fame.
Desire to make Jesus Christ known,
Pray that others may salvation own.
He gave His life, a ransom for many.
No one is exempt, not any.

In Christ are rich treasures.
We forsake earthly pleasures.
Pour out your life until the last drop.
Our motivation to serve the Lord will not stop.
Serve the Lord with all your heart.
From His commandments, do not part.
When we serve, it is for the Lord, not man.
May sinful lives be changed; that is God's plan.
The Lord is continually reforming.
Into His likeness, we are transforming.

The Satisfaction in a Consecrated Life

"And I will very gladly spend and be spent for you;"

11 CORINTHIANS 12:15a

Spend and be spent to win others;
The saved are our sisters and brothers.
Our lives are not our own.
Be wholly yielded to Christ alone.
There is no one exempt from God's concern.
Identify with Jesus; for Him yearn.
What would Jesus do today?
Lord, please help us to obey.
Oh Lord, we will love You exceedingly.
You will send help speedily.

With Christ, we are crucified,
Therefore we are wholly sanctified.
We will be forever content,
When, for Him, our lives are spent.
In Christ, we delight.
Choose to walk in His light.
Be a partner with Jesus in the harvest field.
Share His presence and, to the Holy Spirit, yield.
We must not be a self-defender.
Instead, to Jesus we surrender.

We Empty Ourselves to Serve Others

"though the more abundantly I love you,
the less I be loved."

11 CORINTHIANS 12:15b

To spend and be spent is a joy;
We will bless and not annoy.
To be a servant of all is great.
Do acts of kindness; do not wait.
He became poor for our sakes.
A true disciple gives, not takes.
A faithful witness is committed.
We love Christ and others. That is admitted.
We will delight in the fight for lost souls.
A true disciple, the Lord's name extols.

Be an encouragement,
Not a discouragement.
From sin's bondage we're released.
Selfish, worldly efforts have ceased.
For God's perfect will we yearn.
We expect nothing in return.
Why do we do acts of kindness;
do we look for reward?
Give for the Lord's glory; don't hold back and hoard.
It is with God that we will confer.
What is truth? To the Word, we refer.

Don't Doubt the Excellence of Jesus

"Jesus answered and said unto her, 'If thou knewest
the gift of God, and who it is that saith to thee, Give
me to drink; thou wouldest have asked of Him, and
He would have given thee living water.'"

JOHN 4:10

Our Lord imparts His strength upon us.
Our flesh is weak, but we trust Jesus.
When God is in it,
We're sure to win it!
Let the living waters flow.
His power you will know.
Trust in Him; He is superior.
Our pious self must be inferior.
Where do we get living water?
God supplies each son and daughter.

The water of life has God as its source.
It springs from within and stays on course.
Be put to use.
Laziness, refuse.
Trust Him each day.
Listen and obey!
God gives us living water from His well.
It springs from within; now go and tell.
When we trust self, we are disabled.
Through Christ, we are enabled.

Not From the Wells of Human Nature

"The woman saith unto Him, 'Sir, thou hast nothing
to draw with, and the well is deep; from whence then
hast thou that living water?'"

JOHN 4:11

Our help comes from the Lord of love,
Not from within self, but from above.
The Lord, our God, is Almighty.
Evil things and deeds are flighty.
Our Father is rich and never poor.
This all-powerful sovereign, we adore.
Even when we think our trials have doubled,
Jesus does not want our hearts to be troubled.
In the Lord, we will abide,
Living water He will provide.

Shun the strife;
Have abundant life.
The water Jesus gives,
Heals and loves and lives.
A sinful life must be changed,
It is, by Christ, exchanged.
The Almighty God will never fail.
Fresh water from His well must prevail.
Jesus is our comfort; He does care and sympathize.
He gives; God's divine power we recognize.

Do You Regard the Word As Truth?

"'Now are we sure that Thou knowest all things, and needest not that any man should ask thee: by this we believe that Thou camest forth from God.' Jesus answered them, 'Do ye now believe?'"

JOHN 16:30-31

Let us walk, not in the flesh, but in the Spirit.
God speaks; His Word is truth; hear it!
Come to Jesus; He will lead.
He guides our steps and hears each plead.
The resurrection life of Jesus prevails.
As we rely on Him, His grace avails.
Christ will help us do each task.
He accomplishes, when we ask.
Our Lord is all-knowing.
May His light be forever glowing.

Faith has revived; we are steadfast.
Jesus is Lord; we believe at last!
If we believe, we obey.
Walk in the light each day.
Obedience is right.
Let our fears take flight.
Let not healthy lifestyles be neglected.
Remember, Christ is resurrected.
In everything, God's counsel we seek.
Commonsense decisions can be very weak.

Let Me See Your Light

"Saying, 'What wilt thou that I shall do unto thee?'
And he said, 'Lord, that I may receive my sight.'"

LUKE 18:41

Open our eyes, Lord that we may see,
The blessings You give for Your glory.
God works in supernatural ways.
Ask big; He will amaze!
In Christ, we can do all things.
Blessing and honor and praise He brings.
The blind shall see; the lame shall walk.
Of His amazing grace, we will talk.
God enables us to do each task.
All things are possible; just ask.

Ask of God; He has the ability.
He will do the impossibility.
God's ways are mighty and stupendous.
We can be awestruck; His power is tremendous.
Christ has set us free and we will bring Him glory.
Love and devotion overflows
as we tell the gospel story.
From good thoughts, good ideas come.
Wisdom is action; avoid the humdrum.
To be only human make no exemption.
Authority is ours through His redemption.

March

Awake up, my glory; awake, psaltery and harp: I myself will awake early. I will praise thee, O Lord, among the people: I will sing unto thee among the nations. Psalm 57:8-9

Sticking to the Search for Truth

"So when they had dined, Jesus saith to Simon Peter, 'Simon, son of Jonas, lovest thou Me more than these? He saith unto Him, 'Yea, Lord; thou knowest that I love thee.' He saith unto him, 'Feed My lambs.'"

JOHN 21:15

Love the Lord with heart, soul and mind.
A purer love we cannot find.
We show our love by what we do.
His life, He demonstrates through you.
Confess your love by word and deed.
To the enemy's promptings, don't give heed.
If we love Him, we will feed His sheep.
God loves us; a watch He does keep.
We will show our love and be forever true.
Step by step, He will renew.

The Word of God is the Spirit's sword.
Repentance and faith is our blessed reward.
The Word of the Lord is sharp and will pierce.
Let it fall on receptive ears.
To Christ, our lives are relinquished.
Our lives are yielded to Him;
selfishness is extinguished.
Live only for Christ.
His life has sufficed.
When living in sin, feelings are blunted.
The sword of the Spirit we will use when confronted.

Rejection Brings Dejection

"He saith unto him the second time, 'Simon, son of
Jonas, lovest thou Me'? He saith unto Him, 'Yea,
Lord; thou knowest that I love thee.' He saith unto
him, 'Feed My sheep.'"

JOHN 21:16

Commitment to the LORD must be complete.
Trusting in self is obsolete.
Do you love the Lord with all your heart?
This piercing question He does impart.
He wants us to realize,
He's number One and He is wise.
Lord, search our hearts and You will see.
We love You, increasingly.
Our true natures, He does reveal.
Show your love by kindly deeds; they are His appeal.

When we see there is a need,
His sheep, we will feed.
If we truly love Him,
There is nothing else above Him.
God knows; He loves; He cares.
His mercy and His grace, He shares.
On this premise we can rest.
God gives us only what is best.
Some earthly comforts may be taken away.
We will trust in the Lord, for He is our stay.

The Intensified Search

"He saith unto him the third time, 'Simon, son of
Jonas, lovest thou Me'? Peter was grieved because
He said unto him the third time, 'Lovest thou Me?'
And he said unto Him, 'Lord, thou knowest all things;
thou knowest that I love Thee'. Jesus saith unto him,
'Feed My sheep.'"

JOHN 21:17

Nothing compares with love divine.
In Christ, He has made His love yours and mine.
He sends us out and not to sleep.
A careful watch, the Lord does keep.
Through Christ, His love is manifest.
We follow Him for He knows what is best.
God's love through us is shown.
Witness to others; make the Word known.
The love of God, in Christ, is natural.
He equips us with the supernatural.

Whatever we nourish,
Is bound to flourish.
The good Shepherd, a watch does keep.
His desire is that we feed His sheep.
Those who hunger must be fed.
Be always, by the Spirit, led.
Many sheep have gone astray.
How much more we need to pray.
Jesus' goal has come in view.
To His commission, we must be true.

What Am I Really Living For?

"But none of these things move me, neither count
I my life dear unto myself, so that I might finish my
course with joy, and the ministry, which I have
received of the Lord Jesus, to testify the Gospel of the
grace of God."

ACTS 20:24

God plants a vision in our heart.
We are on His mission; we'll never part.
We count dear what God desires.
A yielded heart, our Lord requires.
Go and tell is God's commission,
We respond with true submission.
We belong to Him; we'll do His will.
We've come, His purpose to fulfill.
With joy, in Christ, we will finish the race.
He's right there to help us in each trial we face.

When we pray and obey, remember the goal.
We testify of God's grace; we may reach a soul.
God's love is our treasure.
It is much too great to measure.
God has given special gifts.
Use them to give spiritual lifts.
The Father's will is what counts.
Give Him glory; He surmounts.
Let this confession be admitted.
Jesus Christ will guide and we are committed.

Who Is On the Throne of Your Heart?

"But none of these things move me, neither count
I my life dear unto myself, so that I might finish my
course with joy, and the ministry, which I have
received of the Lord Jesus, to testify the Gospel of the
grace of God."

ACTS 20:24

To call Him Lord, we must trust and obey.
Find your corner to go forth day by day.
We will share the Good News in song and verse.
Be loyal to Him for better or worse.
Is He really Lord of all your heart?
Trust and obey; He will do His part.
We'll follow Him; we must be fervent.
In hopes one day He'll reward His servant.
He gives opportunity to finish the course.
We will do what He does endorse.

If we love Him, we feed His sheep.
The Great Shepherd, a watch does keep.
To You, Lord, we yield.
Show us the harvest field.
Into the world we are sent.
For Him, our lives are spent.
Totally, to Him, our lives we'll avail.
We know that Jesus will not fail.
The world has a way that will corrupt.
Trust fully in the Spirit to interrupt.

Worthless Events and Belongings

"But in all things approving ourselves as the ministers
of God, in much patience, in afflictions, in necessities,
in distresses,"

11 CORINTHIANS 6:4

One step at a time, the Lord leads.
In prayer, trust and devotion, He meets our needs.
Though daily tasks may seem mundane,
My eyes on Jesus will remain.
You are our vision Lord; we will be fervent.
We are not to live a life of ease; be a servant.
Serve one another in humility.
The Holy Spirit gives us ability.
Love for God will keep on growing,
Love for others will be showing.

May our utmost desire,
Be to excite and inspire.
Our Lord is forever near.
Go forth and persevere.
Bless and refresh those you meet.
In this way, we wash their feet.
Be a source of joy and enlightenment to others.
Be especially kind to your sisters and brothers.
Our salvation, through Christ, we will not neglect.
Day by day our lives He will cleanse and perfect.

Fearless Splendor

"Nay, in all these things we are more than conquerors
through Him that loved us."

ROMANS 8:37

There is nothing between; God is ever-present.
We're full of joy; He is our anti-depressant.
We did not deserve His sacrifice made on the cross.
He came to deliver; our sin is the cause.
We cannot earn the love God gives.
We are super-victorious, because Jesus lives.
Through Christ, our Lord, we're on the winning side.
In the midst of trials, in Him we confide.
The love of God is in our midst.
Sin and sorrow are dismissed.

He makes us strong.
He gives us a song.
From God's love we won't be parted.
His grace and mercy He has imparted.
We sometimes meet contradictions.
Our Lord heals us from afflictions.
Our joy is abundant; He is our source.
The Spirit is gentle; He does not force.
In the midst of trying circumstances,
God's love and grace are perfect; life, He enhances.

The Yielded Spirit

"I am crucified with Christ: nevertheless I live; yet not
I, but Christ liveth in me: and the life which I now live
in the flesh I live by the faith of the Son of God, who
loved me, and gave Himself for me."

GALATIANS 2:20

To be one with Christ, self is crucified.
With all sin laid on Him, we will not be denied.
To His perfect will we yield.
Make us workers in Your field.
We have nothing to bring to God, but our sin.
That is why we need Jesus within.
Be spiritually fit for what He requires.
Through it all, He fulfills our desires.
Die to self each day.
Pride, be gone is what we pray.

We need no longer be a loner.
Christ, the Lord, is our atoner.
Life is so grand.
He takes our hand.
We are God's purchased possession.
He is Lord and that is our confession.
God equips us for each task He has assigned.
We commit to Him our body, soul and mind.
Receive and welcome Him; rely on His name.
Seek first His kingdom and make it your aim.

The Wasted Time of Falling Back

"Then said Jesus unto the twelve,
'Will ye also go away?'"

JOHN 6:67

The secret of joy is to walk in His presence.
Step by step He leads; in Him is sweet essence.
Be set apart to Him alone.
There is no greater calling known.
Trusting the Lord will be our venture.
Our sanctified life is an adventure.
With Jesus Christ, we are one.
He completes the work He has begun.
The uncommitted take their leave.
We must forever to Jesus cleave.

Will you stay or will you depart?
Grace and mercy our Lord does impart.
On Jesus Christ we can depend.
Our devotion to Him should never end.
The Spirit gives life.
He frees us from strife.
Don't turn back.
In Christ there's no lack.
What, in fact, has the best appeal?
Our Lord Jesus Christ is alive and real.

Give It and Live It

"Preach the Word; be instant in season, out of
season; reprove, rebuke, exhort with all long-suffering
and doctrine."

11 TIMOTHY 4:2

Our lives are letters to be read.
We are children of God; by Christ, we are led.
Speak forth the message, loud and clear.
What do they see and what do they hear?
Declare what you know to be true.
New life and purpose we will renew.
Correct, rebuke and inspire.
Instruct carefully; lift faith higher.
Preach the Word in every season.
Scripture is God-breathed, that's the reason.

The Bible is open; His Word we declare.
Preach the Gospel everywhere.
May what we do
Say I love you.
We watch carefully what we say.
It can help someone along the way.
Let your life be a holy example.
Christ is the message; He is ample.
Don't just give a testimony; reflect the Son.
Faith, in action produces deeds well done.

Seeing Beyond

"Whereupon, O king Agrippa, I was not disobedient
unto the heavenly vision."

ACTS 26:19

The plan and purpose of God is forever upheld.
The blessings He promised will not be withheld.
Without a vision, the people perish.
Eternal life is what we cherish.
The test is in the here and now.
The Lord will show us how.
Be constant as the foresight you recall.
Moment by moment, give Him your all.
We must not lose sight of God's purpose.
The Lord has sent us; He gives us impetus.

As a faithful servant,
May each one of us be fervent.
In the midst of a storm,
Our hearts to Him will conform.
Oh Lord, help us to obey.
Trust Him every minute of every day.
We behold God's glory and repent.
When cleansed and refreshed, we will not relent.
God's glory is great; we are so sinful and small.
He grants us forgiveness and sends us to tell all.

Surrender

"Then Peter began to say unto Him, 'Lo, we have left
all, and have followed Thee.'"

MARK 10:28

We abandon ourselves to the cross.
In Christ, we will suffer no loss.
It is the Lord, alone, we worship.
There is no greater fellowship.
Oh Lord, it is You that we desire.
Let our selfish interests expire.
Our love for the Lord is unrestrained.
From earthly lusts, we are refrained.
In Christ, there is no lack.
To follow Him, hold nothing back.

Oh Lord, we know You are our defender.
Unto You, we will surrender.
We surrender all.
We will not fall.
Go for the goal.
Give your heart, mind and soul.
Worldly quest may leave us hollow.
It is Jesus, we will follow.
Yielded lives to Christ must be complete.
No longer with the world will we compete.

He Gave His All

"For God so loved the world that He gave His only
begotten Son, that whosoever believeth in Him should
not perish, but have everlasting life."

JOHN 3:16

God gave completely His all.
Proclaim liberty; we will not fall.
God has delivered and set us free.
Jesus gave His life for you and me.
What are we called to proclaim?
Salvation is only in Jesus' name.
The gift of God is absolute.
He came to save the destitute.
Those who trust in Christ are fully assured.
God proclaims it in His Word.

Reckon self to be dead and enter into His union.
We thank You, Lord, for sweet communion.
Selfishness will not be prominent.
The Lord Jesus Christ is dominant.
Give Him your all.
You will stand tall.
Have a satisfactory effect,
Your relationship with the Lord, perfect.
Jesus Christ shed His blood for our sins.
The battle is in the Spirit and the true believer wins.

Submit? To Whom

"Know ye not, that to whom ye yield yourselves
servants to obey, his servants ye are to whom ye
obey; whether of sin unto death, or of obedience unto
righteousness?"

ROMANS 6:16

Unto God, let our spirits yield.
He wants us to glean in His field.
We must not give in to lust.
Christ delivers; He is just.
Let Jesus be your Lord and Master;
He will keep you from disaster.
To whom are you obedient?
Yield to Jesus; that's expedient.
Will you yield to God's will today?
His servant you are to whom you obey.

Our faith is sealed.
To the Spirit, we will yield.
Who is in control?
In Christ, be made whole.
Forget not to pray for other's needs.
Respond, in faith, to their earnest pleads.
In the midst of trials, do not fret.
Express the love of Jesus; don't forget.
With lust for worldly goods, be not obsessed.
Fix thoughts on God's purpose as faith is professed.

Submission to God

"And they were in the way going up to Jerusalem; and
Jesus went before them; and they were amazed; and
as they followed, they were afraid. And He took again
the twelve, and began to tell them what things should
happen unto Him,"

MARK 10:32

The sinless life of Jesus amazes.
The love of God, in Christ, embraces.
Within the darkness of dismay,
Jesus brightens up each day.
We know not where He will bring us.
He wants us to follow and not make a fuss.
Be devoted and obedient to His cause.
You'll not be upset nor suffer loss.
Worship and praise may be filled with true emotion.
What God desires is a heart of devotion.

Commit to His demands.
Submit to His commands.
Do not become alarmed.
In the Holy Spirit, we are fully armed.
It is an awesome kind of fear,
To know that our Lord is near.
Lord, what will You have us do today?
We will follow You and walk Your way.
We can turn back, or we can walk ahead.
Walk away from sinful acts; walk with Jesus, instead.

Our Lord Judges Rightly

"For we must all appear before the judgment seat of Christ; that every one may receive the things done in his body, according to that he hath done, whether it be good or bad."

II CORINTHIANS 5:10

At the judgment seat we must appear.
When Christ is within, we need not fear.
Live in holiness; walk in the light.
The Spirit convicts; He helps us to do right.
Immediately, confess a fault.
Walk in the light; the Lord exalt.
Our good and bad deeds are assessed.
Intentional sin must be confessed.
We will all be judged; there are no exceptions.
Be alert for the Spirit's interceptions.

On the day of reward, our lives are resounded.
Oh, may our lives in the Word be
rooted and grounded.
May the day of reckoning bring delight.
We will serve the Lord with all our might.
Requital day must come for all.
Repent; be ready; on Jesus call.
In the heavenly court, our lives will be reviewed.
It is a time of praising; our lives have been renewed.
Day by day our hearts are at peace and we are glad.
It is only in Christ that we are righteously clad.

Labors of Love

"Wherefore we labor, that whether present or absent,
we may be accepted of Him."

II CORINTHIANS 5:9

Christ, the Lord; this is our desire.
He shed His blood. He is the salvation supplier.
God will keep us from disaster.
We look to Him as our Lord and Master.
May our satisfying desire be kept right.
Keep God's standards in your sight.
We hope to never face rejection.
To Him, we'll remain in subjection.
We are with the Lord by faith, not sight.
Therefore, we will love Him with all our might.

He is our passion.
He sets the fashion.
Avoid the enemy's teasing.
Be, to God, well-pleasing.
Clearly aim without distraction.
Jesus is our main attraction.
To be accepted in the Beloved is our goal.
He has cleansed and made us whole.
Lord, of Your presence, may we be aware; appoint us.
Your Word of truth we will share, when You anoint us.

Wake Up to God's Perfection

"Having therefore these promises, dearly beloved, let us cleanse ourselves from all filthiness of the flesh and spirit, perfecting holiness in the fear of God."

II CORINTHIANS 7:1

Cleanse our hearts, O God, and make them pure.
The Temple must be sanctified for sure.
God, the Son, is found in you and me.
We will walk and talk in purity.
Watch and pray; constantly submit.
Jesus is Lord is what we will admit.
In obedience, life is transformed.
Submit to Him and be conformed.
In everything, we will put God first.
He cleanses us; for Him we thirst.

Sin and self-centeredness, we do forsake.
God's marvelous grace we take.
In Christ be complete.
Don't retreat.
It is Him we want to know.
Fully trusting, we will grow.
This is the best way that we can operate:
With God, we will cooperate.
Worldly paths lead to destruction.
We must heed to God's instruction.

Believe and Receive

"By faith Abraham, when he was called to go out into
a place which he should after receive for an
inheritance, obeyed; and he went out, not knowing
whither he went."

HEBREWS 11:8

Love the Lord more than any other.
Be more devoted to Him than to sister or brother.
To be like Jesus is our aim.
We look not to success or fame.
We want to go where our Master leads.
As we step out in faith, He meets our needs.
Faith and obedience go hand in hand.
Upon God's Word we take our stand.
When we have faith, we walk, not faint.
Our Lord Jesus Christ equips each saint.

With God, our Father, we're related.
We are from the worldly ways separated.
He is the life giver.
Each Christian will be a faith liver.
Receive the goal:
It is salvation of the soul.
Believers are shielded by God's power.
Faith and grace avail this hour.
He has called us to His glory and virtue now.
The Holy Spirit will lead and show us how.

An Intimate Supporter of Jehovah

"And the LORD said, 'Shall I hide from Abraham that thing which I do; seeing that Abraham shall surely become a great and mighty nation, and all the nations of the earth shall be blessed in him?'"

GENESIS 18:17-18

In Christ we are free, liberated and delighted.
The Holy Spirit's pure vision is not blighted.
Continue to pray till the answer comes.
If the Lord refuses, the urging succumbs.
We ask, in faith, believing.
What God desires, is what we're receiving.
Go God's way; do what is right and just.
Desire His will; in Him put your trust.
Our desire is to be in one accord:
This is the will of our loving Lord.

When praying, do not stop short.
Let the answer be a good report.
In Christ, we are free.
We live in victory.
In Him, delight,
Do what is right.
Live a life of freedom, liberty and gladness.
The Lord helps us to be released from our sadness.
Difficulties may come tomorrow.
We can have joy in the midst of sorrow.

Attention or As Certainty

"Knowing this, that our old man is crucified with Him,
that the body of sin might be destroyed, that
henceforth we should not serve sin."

ROMANS 6:6

Dead to self and alive in Christ!
He gave His life; that has sufficed.
Jesus shed His blood for you and me.
He gave His all to set us free.
To our Lord, we are committed.
Our Redeemer lives; we have admitted.
Christ, our Savior lives within the heart.
Surrender to Him; He will not depart.
With whom are we identified?
Abide in Christ; He is glorified.

To Christ, our Lord, we call for aid.
He, alone, for our sins paid.
Please be advised:
To live is Christ!
In the flesh, we are no longer;
In Christ, we are stronger.
Carnal chains are flung away.
We will trust in Christ each day.
Christ paid the price so we can be free.
Of this fact, we will agree.

Aflame With Warm Affection

"And they said one to another, 'Did not our heart burn
within us, while He talked with us by the way, and
while He opened to us the Scriptures?'"

LUKE 24:32

All is sufficient when, in Christ, we abide.
We have no fear; in Him we hide.
Christ appears with wonderful visions.
He sends us on compelling missions.
Did you receive light on the mountain?
Let the living water flow like a fountain.
He walks with us along the way.
He opens the Scriptures yet today.
Along the journey, He gives direction.
We walk with Him under His protection.

Refrain from depression;
Share faith with expression.
In the presence of the Lord we dwell.
The Good News of the Gospel we will tell.
Within us, our hearts are burning.
For His steadfast presence be ever-yearning.
The guest at our table has become our host.
Our hearts burn within us; we love Him the most.
Mundane tasks can sometimes cause us to be bored.
We need not be sorrowful; we walk with the Lord.

Am I Opposed to the Spiritual?

"For ye are yet carnal: for whereas there is among
you envying, and strife, and divisions, are ye not
carnal, and walk as men?"

I CORINTHIANS 3:3

Jealousy and strife are at odds with the Spirit.
When sanctified wholly, we need not fear it.
The Spirit calls: Accept the light.
He will make things turn out right.
We must give up carnal ways.
The light of God will fill our days.
Do you for completeness long?
Confess, forsake; God rights the wrong.
What are the attributes of a resurrected life?
We must have no part of jealousy and strife.

The Holy Spirit keeps us from doing wrong,
Because with the Lord we are strong.
Against carnal ways, we must fight.
In our new nature, there is delight.
There is a battle: flesh or Spirit?
Walk in God's path; do not fear it.
The grace of God makes us fit and able.
The flesh is defeated; the Spirit is stable.
In the Word of God, the Christian finds contentment.
The heart of the believer harbors no resentment.

Become Less, for He is More

"He must increase, but I must decrease."

JOHN 3:30

We can lead to water, but they must do the drinking.
As they look to Jesus, His thoughts they'll be thinking.
Our own cravings and desires diminish.
Christ is on the throne to the finish.
Our love for Jesus will grow and grow.
The Bridegroom cares more than we will ever know.
Each one must, to the Lord, be true.
Daily, we will faith renew.
We must be humble; Jesus is greater.
Seek Him first; He's the Creator.

Let our stubborn wills decrease.
May God's perfect will increase.
We are united to Christ, that we may bear fruits.
Be planted firmly in faith; down deep are our roots.
We are the Bridegroom's friend.
Our friendship with the Lord will not end.
He was raised from the dead, that we might bear fruit.
To feed on what He has provided is a healthy pursuit.
Rejoice when those you love, on the Lord, depend.
Release them to His care; Jesus loves each friend.

Our Perspective? Lift up Jesus!

"He that hath the bride is the Bridegroom; but the friend of the Bridegroom, which standeth and heareth Him, rejoiceth greatly because of the Bridegroom's voice; my joy therefore is fulfilled."

JOHN 3:29

Let us lift up and magnify Jesus.
It is He, alone, that will please us.
With Christ, we will be inter-active.
This, to others, is attractive.
We must decrease; He must increase.
His love and mercy will never cease.
Magnify Jesus more and more.
He is the One that we adore.
With Jesus Christ, we remain connected.
He lives within; He is resurrected.

The Bridegroom must be on center stage.
Draw others to Christ; in this engage.
On Christ, we will rely.
His power, we can't deny
We are, to the Son of God, related.
This should not be understated.
Let not others, on you, be dependant.
As they grow in grace, they can become independent.
Moral and vital relationship with Christ is essential.
Friendship with the Bridegroom is providential.

The Foresight of Individual Innocence

"Blessed are the pure in heart;
for they shall see God."

MATTHEW 5:8

Perfect us, Lord, by Your purity.
Only in You is there holy security.
Look not at a person's faults.
Christ protects us from the enemy's assaults.
With our personal Savior, we are in one accord.
For personal purity, He must be our Lord.
How do they know we love Jesus much?
It is by what we do and what we touch.
Our inner sanctuary must be kept pure.
God gives us grace, so we may endure.

As we press on,
May we reveal the Son.
Are we entirely pure?
Christ does cleanse and ensure.
In purity, we will grow.
His sovereign grace, He does bestow.
Our perfection is in Christ Jesus alone.
Our lives should make His presence known.
In the Lord's abiding presence, joy is complete.
We need not with the world compete.

Walking on Higher Ground

"After this, I looked, and behold, a door was opened in heaven: and the first voice which I heard was as it were of a trumpet talking with me; which said, 'Come up hither, and I will show thee things which must be hereafter.'"

REVELATION 4:1

We are seated in the heavenly places.
We will walk wholly in His graces.
In the vastness of God's tableland,
We are safe. On higher ground we stand.
Jesus is the solid Rock.
We are secure in Him and not amok.
To grow in grace is our desire.
He commands us to come up higher.
Stand true to the Lord and in Him be found.
He will lift you up to higher ground.

To be in heavenly places is our goal.
We learn God's graces; He saves our soul.
It is the Lord that we adore.
We want to know Him more and more.
How can we be filled?
We must do what God has willed.
Be not bogged down with doubts and complaints.
God reveals His purpose to His saints.
From heaven's throne; holiness, He sends.
He gives grace and deliverance to His friends.

Do We Interpret Wrongly?

"Then after that saith He to His disciples, 'Let us go
into Judea again.' His disciples say unto Him,
'Master, the Jews of late sought to stone Thee; and
goest Thou thither again?'"

JOHN 11:7-8

There is a battle with submission.
Lord, help us fulfill Your great commission.
In obedience, we bring Him glory.
He implores us to preach and teach the gospel story.
The Word of God commands us to do what is right.
God's honor is our great delight.
The orders He gives are good and kind.
When He says we should do it, we are to mind.
Whatever He says to you, do it.
Have you broken a vow? Renew it.

His glory is shown to all who observe.
From his pathway do not swerve.
Oh Lord, our faith, renew.
What You speak, we will do.
God answers when we pray.
He directs our paths each day.
The Lord compels us.
Do what He tells us.
The Lord wants us to launch out.
We must believe Him and not doubt.

Jesus Comes; Be Ready!

"Be ye therefore ready also; for the Son of man
cometh at an hour when ye think not."

LUKE 12:40

Moment by moment and at every turn,
Christ is present; from Him we will learn.
We meet the Lord at every corner.
Be encouraged and not a mourner.
Our expectation must be steady.
He appears suddenly; be ready.
Your love and devotion to Christ must be real.
Genuine faith has great appeal.
Don't trust in religion; be spiritually real.
Keep your eyes on Jesus, and follow with zeal.

Faith must be vital.
Jesus is our recital.
Our Lord's visits may surprise us.
He is right there to advise us.
Always remember; He is right there.
He lifts your burden and answers your prayer.
Some gatherings may be difficult to attend.
Be at one with the Lord; we will not offend.
Be watching; He can come at any moment.
The Word of God is true; His return is imminent.

Divinity vs. Division

"And He saw that there was no man, and wondered
that there was no intercessor: therefore His arm
brought salvation unto Him; and His righteousness, it
sustained Him."

ISAIAH 59:16

God calls us to intercede.
He will answer every need.
Worship and have the mind of Christ.
His intercession has sufficed.
Our prayers should not be artificial.
A prayer from the heart is beneficial.
The Church needs revival and salvation.
We will stand in the gap with determination.
What wonderful things, through prayer, are wrought.
We will pray; these blessings can't be bought.

He hears and this, we declare.
Of our requests, He is aware.
We make our plea for each spiritual need.
He will answer as we plead.
Our selfish wants and wishes scatter.
We ask Him what His will is in this matter.
When our Lord intercedes,
justice is served.
We walk in victory and are no longer unnerved.
The Word of the LORD is true and tried.
His divine instruction should not be cast aside.

Attentiveness or Assumption

"And this is the confidence that we have in Him, that,
if we ask any thing according to His will, He heareth
us: And if we know that He hear us, whatsoever we
ask, we know that we have the petitions that we
desired of Him."

I JOHN 5:14-15

Lord, help us not to criticize,
All are precious in God's eyes.
Pray, instead, for those who err.
May God be worshipped everywhere.
Worship the Lord; then entreat.
He changes people and makes us complete.
Put God first in every situation.
When one with Him, He brings salvation.
Forgive us, Lord, for our lack of interest.
May Your divine power be made manifest.

Do you see a soul in need?
Have sympathy; pray and plead.
Friends may be in fearful destitution,
God can heal them of their confusion.
Needs of others are discerned.
Let them know you are concerned.
For each trial we face,
God administers grace.
The needs of others are anticipated.
May they have faith and be emancipated.

April

And I will make them and the places round about my hill a blessing; and I will cause the shower to come down in his season; there shall be showers of blessing. Ezekiel 34:26

Warmth vs. Coolness Toward Others

"Who is He that condemneth? It is Christ that died,
yea rather, that is risen again, Who is even at the right
hand of God, Who also maketh intercession for us."
(27) "And He that searcheth the hearts knoweth what
is the mind of the Spirit, because He maketh
intercession for the saints
according to the will of God."

ROMANS 8:34 & 27

Though some circumstances will not please us,
Prayer changes things; call on Jesus.
True compassion stems from the heart.
The love Jesus has, He does impart.
Oh, how we long to do His will.
With agape love, He will fulfill.
Christ lives forever; He is omnipresent.
He is the believer's antidepressant.
The Spirit inspires and empowers the saints.
He is aware of all our needs and complaints.

We can have confidence in prayer.
Our comforter is with us everywhere.
We may see a need.
It is then that we intercede.
Friendship is nice;Take God's advice.
We may choose to help or to walk away.
We must trust the Lord and pray.
Kindly deeds may become our fascination.
Put God first in every situation.

The Height of Excellence

"And Ananias went his way, and entered into the
house; and putting his hands on him said, 'Brother
Saul, the Lord, even Jesus, that appeared unto thee
in the way as thou camest, hath sent me, that thou
mightest receive thy sight, and be
filled with the Holy Ghost.'"

ACTS 9:17

Open our eyes, Lord, and let us see.
You died and arose to set us free.
This is the thing we want to know.
God's glory and grace He does bestow.
To Jesus Christ we are attracted
We are not by evil ways distracted.
Oh Lord, may we receive our sight.
Only You will be our Light.
A man after God's own heart will be filled.
His mercy and grace, to us, is instilled.

Be filled with the Spirit and willing to serve.
From God's pathway, refuse to swerve.
With Christ in our vision,
We are sent on a mission.
We have received our sight.
We trust the Lord with all our might.
Our spiritual eyes are opened to see:
The glory of Christ gives victory.
Good News should be spread to every nation.
Blind eyes are made to see and receive salvation.

New Insight Relieves Old Mistakes

"Saying, 'If thou hadst known, even thou, at least in
this thy day, the things which belong unto thy peace!
but now they are hid from thine eyes.'"

LUKE 19:42

In life's circumstances we are taught.
Pride of religion is put to naught.
Let not pride appear as white-washed.
Let your heart and life be blood-washed.
We cannot undo what has been done.
Upon God's path we have begun.
Jesus wept over those who are lost.
He was willing and paid the cost.
We need to know what makes for peace.
We are free in Christ; He brings release.

Learn from each past mistake.
Today, go forth, for Glory's sake.
The past is gone;
We must carry on.
Sometimes we shut doors in error.
It is then that we may meet with terror.
Many lessons of life, we have learned.
Teach us today; God's guidance is discerned.
What might have been needed not be troublesome.
Past failures strengthen us and help us to overcome.

On the Edge of Suspicion

"Behold the hour cometh, yea, is now come, that ye
shall be scattered, every man to his own, and shall
leave me alone: and yet I am not alone, because the
Father is with me."

JOHN 16:32

Be at work in things that matter,
Let there be no idleness and silly chatter.
God puts circumstances in our path.
We overcome; He frees from wrath.
Wherever we go, whatever we do,
You are Lord and You'll see us through.
We can praise and thank God that all is well.
He knows our needs before we tell.
Jesus Christ is Lord; our faith is real.
We follow Him; our hearts, He will heal.

When our own feelings are denied,
That is when we are sanctified.
When a disappointing event scatters,
We find it is God that really matters.
We exercise faith in each encounter.
Christ, Himself, is our surmounter.
Life is full of mixed up pieces,
We need a relationship with Jesus.
Our faith is what will last forever.
In God we trust; from this we will not sever.

His Pangs and Our Companionship

"Then cometh Jesus with them unto a place called Gethsemane, and saith unto the disciples, 'Sit ye here, while I go and pray yonder.' Then saith He unto them, 'My soul is exceeding sorrowful, even unto death: tarry ye here, and watch with Me.'"

MATTHEW 26:36 & 38

Jesus came to pay the price.
For sin, He was the sacrifice.
The garden and the cross lead to life.
He has delivered from sin and strife.
Jesus Christ won the victory,
He gave His life upon the tree.
The Son of God came on purpose to die.
On His redemption we must rely.
Gethsemane and Calvary are the gateway to life.
Christ triumphs over sin and frees us from strife.

The price has been paid.
His life down He laid.
Sin, He became.
He took our shame
Christ did agonize.
He paid the sacrifice.
The tomb is empty in accord with God's plan.
Christ died for our sins;
He arose and is coming again.
Jesus prayed to get through the Father's plan.
His death and resurrection brought new life to man.

The Impact of Jehovah and Iniquity

"Who His own self bare our sins in His own body on the tree, that we, being dead to sins, should live unto righteousness: by whose stripes ye were healed."

I PETER 2:24

In the cross of Jesus Christ we glory.
He paid in full; spread the Gospel story.
Christ bared our sins upon the cross.
As redeemed saints, we fear no loss.
The cross is a place of victory.
Our union with Him is not contradictory.
He took our sins upon Himself and paid the price.
His own blood was the supreme sacrifice.
His blood was shed upon the tree.
He suffered there for you and me.

Behold the empty tomb.
He lives! We know for sure and do not just assume.
Christ died and rose again.
He lives in us; Hallelujah, Amen!
Christ has promised to return.
We will trust in Him and will listen and learn.
It was for this purpose that God sent His Son.
He delivers from sin; it is finished; it is done.
Christ was guilty of no sin; He never spoke deceit.
The purpose of His sacrifice was the enemy to defeat.

Spiritual Discernment

"And as they came down from the mountain, He charged them that they should tell no man what things they had seen, till the Son of man were risen from the dead."

MARK 9:9

When life abundant is made real,
Christ within will save and heal.
One with Christ is a blessed union.
We have such precious, sweet communion.
We don't speak with an empty word or deed.
The Risen Christ is our greatest need.
A stubborn attitude must cease.
Only the Living Christ will please.
Our Lord is risen and we proclaim it.
He is risen in us. That's salvation; we will name it.

Jesus Christ was resurrected.
He will come again as expected.
We will understand,
When we hold His hand.
This is our sincere attraction.
Live in us, Lord; let there be no distraction.
We will not be distressed.
In Christ, we are blessed!
He calls us by name; we are put to a test.
Our response to the Lord is that
He knows what is best.

His Resurrection Destiny

"Ought not Christ to have suffered these things, and
to enter into His glory?"

LUKE 24:26

Christ was crucified to give us life.
His peace prevails; He eases strife.
When does this new life begin?
It comes as soon as one is born again!
We can abide in Him this hour,
He gives us His resurrection power.
He bore sin's penalty in our behalf.
In His new life, we love and laugh.
Christ suffered in the flesh and entered His splendor.
He rules and reigns; He is our Defender.

The truth sets us free.
We will live eternally.
Christ has entered His glory.
Often repeat this Gospel story.
The burden for our sins He bears.
To glory, Christ brings many heirs.
By the truth we will know the way to go.
He has given new life and in faith we grow.
Christ said it is finished; the truth, He confessed.
When accused and persecuted, do not be distressed.

Behold His Glory

"After that He appeared in another form unto two of them, as they walked, and went into the country."

MARK 16:12

We will see Jesus.
He alone will please us.
Worldly pleasures have no appeal.
When Jesus appears, His glory He will reveal.
With our eyes on the Lord,
He is fully adored.
When we see Jesus, we want to go His way.
We cannot walk in paths of sin and dismay.
To each individual, He does appear.
Once you have met Him, He is ever near.

Faith is strengthened when He comes on the scene.
Walk in His presence; have nothing between.
Reach for the goal:
It is salvation for the soul.
On Jesus, our eyes are planted.
He gives us the rest that He has granted.
Worldly ways can become a distraction.
The presence of the Lord is our attraction.
Even if others won't believe, we must do right.
Speak forth the Gospel message; let the Spirit incite.

Spiritual Discrimination

"Knowing this, that our old man is crucified with Him,
that the body of sin might be destroyed, that
henceforth we should not serve sin."

ROMANS 6:6

Lord, thank you for a life of victory.
In Christ, we are a new creation and set free.
Flesh and Spirit are incompatible.
Reckon flesh dead, no more to quibble.
Sin in me is put out of service.
Under the blood, God does dismiss.
Slavery to sin has been broken.
It is finished. The Word has been spoken.
Be no longer, by sin, annoyed.
The body of sin has been destroyed.

The big I in sin is crucified.
Christ died; and the big I died.
When we make a move,
May our Lord approve.
May self-life be killed.
May the love of Christ be instilled.
Oh, Lord, rule and reign from within each heart.
Help us to do what You accept and from sin, depart.
We need not sin; we have new life and peace.
Be dead to sin and alive to Christ; sinful ways cease.

God is in Charge

"For if we have been planted together in the likeness of His death, we shall be also in the likeness of His resurrection:"

ROMANS 6:5

We have Christ's resurrection life within,
He has cleansed from all sin.
We trust in His redeeming love,
He gives orders from above.
The Holy Spirit does refine,
He makes us morally divine.
To be like You, Lord, is our desire.
The Holy Spirit will inspire.
Walk in the light and obey what He reveals.
With Christ within, sin no longer appeals.

The Holy Spirit puts our lives in order.
We're made in His likeness; He's the awarder.
Sin and sorrow are defective,
New life in Christ is effective.
A Christian life is resurrected.
By the Holy Spirit, we are directed.
Walk in the light and obey what He does reveal.
He will keep us steady and on an even keel.
The Temple of God is holy.
That means that we must be sanctified wholly.

God Dominates From Within

"Knowing that Christ being raised from the dead dieth no more; death hath no more dominion over Him. For in that He died, He died unto sin once: but in that He liveth, He liveth unto God. Likewise reckon ye also yourselves to be dead indeed unto sin, but alive unto God through Jesus Christ our Lord."

ROMANS 6:9-11

The same Spirit that raised Christ from the dead,
Quickens our mortal bodies and gives
new life instead.
Eternal life, the Savior gives.
Our flesh is dead; the Spirit lives!
Be filled with the Holy Spirit's power.
Trust in the Lord; He gives life each hour.
The Lord Jesus Christ is our only source.
He keeps us on the pure and holy course.
Let go and let God do it.
He helps us to get through it.

To sin, we are dead.
We are alive to God instead.
We trust no other opinion.
We let Christ have dominion.
Life, in Christ, is never defective.
In Him, we are complete and effective.
When trusting in self there are many lacks.
Full fellowship with God equips us to relax.
Death has no more power over the Lord's anointed.
When dead to sin, in Christ we're divinely appointed.

Bestow on Him Your Heavy Load

"Cast thy burden upon the LORD, and He shall
sustain thee; He shall never suffer the
righteous to be moved."

PSALMS 55:22

On You, Lord, our burdens are cast.
Anxious uneasiness has passed.
Peace and joy spring forth freely.
Sin and sorrow are not in style, really.
The burden is here, but under control,
He will strengthen and console.
When facing trials too great to bear,
God wants us, on Him, to cast our care.
Bring anxiety to God in prayer.
He bestows His peace; He's everywhere.

He sustains and enables; He is ever-true.
He cares for us and brings us through.
Our sins are confessed.
Our faith is professed.
We agonize with tearful eyes.
Could this burden be a blessing in disguise?
With others, we serve;
From God's pathway, don't swerve.
Every day, His mercies are new.
Always remember that He cares for you.
Heavy hearts are lifted, when the Savior
comes in view.
He carries our load as our faith we renew.

Supernatural Victory

"Take my yoke upon you, and learn of Me;
for I am meek and lowly in heart: and ye shall find
rest unto your souls. For My yoke is easy, and My
burden is light."

MATTHEW 11:29, 30

We will not murmur nor complain.
He bears the yoke and eases pain.
His love expands to any length.
In Him, we have great strength.
His yoke is easy; and His burden is light,
He shares with us His grace and might.
He eases our heavy weights with His grace.
He brings us through each trial we face.
Chastening is a blessing–not a curse.
If we're not corrected, we will behave worse.

One with Christ is a majority.
His leads and guides; He has authority.
As a worker in God's field,
We must, to the Spirit, yield.
In the Lord, we are strong.
We are blessed; we belong!
The burden is too heavy. The enemy does provoke.
Always remember that Jesus bears the yoke.
How do we defeat the enemy's scheme?
There is victory in Jesus; He came to redeem.

A Lapse in Thought

"But the high places were not taken away out of
Israel; nevertheless the heart of Asa was perfect all
his days."

II CHRONICLES 15: 17

With God, everything matters.
Speak the truth; silly talk scatters.
God watches over every detail,
His grace and mercy always prevail.
We have to learn to take our stand,
Hold on tightly to His hand.
Whenever there is fear and doubt,
Plead His blood; we cannot do without.
To the Lord, be fully committed.
Do only that which He's permitted.

Be not negligent,
But be diligent.
Some things must be restricted.
The Holy Spirit has convicted.
Be ever alert to God's plan.
From worldly places, place a ban.
Pay close attention to what brings rest and reposing.
Our high places in life may be God opposing.
Is there something over which you have not obeyed?
Keep yourself fit and be not, by temptations, swayed.

Are You Able to Descend?

"While ye have light, believe in the light that ye may
be the children of light."

JOHN 12:36

A high standard must be lifted up,
Low times try to interrupt.
Unto the Lord, our lives we commit.
When He gives us direction, we will not just sit.
Let's not nullify God's grace by our actions.
Friendship with the world brings many distractions.
Walk in the pathway of His choosing.
Follow Him; you'll not be losing.
When you fail,
Let faith prevail.

Lessons learned on the mountaintop,
In the valley, should not stop.
On the peak times, we know.
It is in the valley that we grow.
When light from above has been revealed,
Walk forward and act on what God has appealed.
When inspired to do a kindness, perform the task.
The Lord will empower giving even more than we ask.
Each waking moment, God's message we promote.
We run the race with joy and our lives to God devote.

God's Way or No Way

"Therefore that disciple whom Jesus loved saith unto
Peter, 'It is the Lord.' Now when Simon Peter heard
that it was the Lord, he girt his fisher's coat unto him
and did cast himself into the sea."

JOHN 21:7

Commitment to Christ is needed.
He makes things all right, when His will is heeded.
Into the sea of life, our lives are cast.
When abandoned to Christ, He holds us fast.
Fully committed, we will be.
We will do His will, deliberately.
We want to reach satisfaction.
We will trust His leading and go into action.
To further the Gospel, we are committed.
He is Lord; this we have admitted.

Plunge into what God does command.
On His truth, take your stand.
Jesus will be your light.
He sets you on a path that is right.
On the name of Jesus, call.
Be ready always to give Him your all.
With anticipation, we welcome this day.
We meet it with joy and not with dismay.
It is God's will; this is our defense.
Leave up to Him the consequence.

Be Prepared

"When the LORD saw that he turned aside to see,
God called unto him out of the midst of the bush, and
said, 'Moses, Moses.' And he said, 'Here am I.'"

EXODUS 3:4

To do Your will, Lord, we are prepared.
Your Word is ready to be shared.
It is in the little things that God works.
His faithful servant never shirks.
To do some deed of kindness, we are ready.
The Unseen Host prods on and keeps us steady.
In His presence, never fear.
When He commands, tell Him you are here.
At the burning bush, ablaze with fire,
A surrendered heart, God does require.

Living in God's presence,
Brings His Light to essence.
Sometimes, from routine, we must part.
Do what God speaks to your heart.
When He calls, say "Here I am!"
From His presence, do not scram.
When, to God, our lives avail,
His divine purpose will not fail.
Be ready always to hear God's instruction.
Heed not to the tales of the enemy's destruction.

To Almighty God Be True

"Then tidings came to Joab; for Joab had turned
after Adonijah, though he turned not after Absalom,
and Joab fled unto the tabernacle of the LORD, and
caught hold on the horns of the altar."

I KINGS 2:28

To the Lord alone be true.
Man will fail; Jesus will renew.
Through storms of life, the battle rages.
God sees us through in many stages.
In His redemptive power we are kept.
Our faith has failed if we have slept.
We depend upon God's power and faithfulness.
We trust in Him with affirmed gratefulness.
Keep alert; keep your memory bright.
Unguarded strength could be your plight.

Meet temptation with meekness.
God's power is demonstrated through weakness.
For the cause of Christ, become a soldier.
The Holy Spirit will make us bolder.
Stay on God's course.
From evil plots, divorce.
To accomplish the task, be diligent.
Move steadily forward; be vigilant.
Let us run the race and determine to win.
Remain true to God and renounce all sin.

Trust Him For the Moment

"For all the promises of God in Him are yea,
and in Him Amen,
unto the glory of God by us."

II CORINTHIANS 1:20

In Him, we are enabled.
Our cant's are tabled.
God's promises are completed in Christ.
The spiritual gifts have sufficed.
Never say, "I can't, Sir."
This is spiritual cancer.
Be ready to stand each trial and test.
The power of God will be manifest.
He fulfills His promises; do not worry.
He's in control; He does not hurry.

Always put God's kingdom first.
For the Holy Spirit, thirst.
Even if our talent is only one,
With it, we can glorify the Son.
We will seek the Lord with all our heart,
From His presence, we will not depart.
Going our own way is a disaster.
Jesus must be our Lord and Master.
Say yes to God; He will supply the need.
Be not complacent; He gives good gifts indeed.

Perfect Trust in His Presence

Jesus saith unto him, 'Have I been so long time with
you, and yet hast thou not known me, Philip? He that
hath seen Me hath seen the Father; and how sayest
thou then, 'Show us the Father?''

JOHN 14:9

God will never leave, nor forsake.
He's always near; reach out and take.
In child-like faith we take His hand,
He will help us understand.
In each circumstance, God is in charge.
Fret not; our faith He will enlarge.
Each one is precious in God's eyes.
He is right here, we realize.
He is ever-present; do not fear.
Call upon Him; He will hear.

Fret not in anxiety and unbelief.
The Lord is always present to give relief.
Unto Him, our lives we commit.
Moment by moment, we submit.
The truth God gives, we will declare.
Our lives to Him entrust and share.
Where we are placed, we won't resent.
We must be aware that our Lord is present.
We will not muster up faith by our intellect.
The Word of God, written on our hearts,
we will select.

His Brightness Will Not Fade

"But we all, with open face beholding as in a glass the glory of the Lord, are changed into the same image from glory to glory, even as by the Spirit of the Lord."

II CORINTHIANS 3:18

We can trust the Lord; He does atone.
He's the only faithful friend we've known.
We need never walk on a crooked path.
Jesus walks with us; He frees us from wrath.
The love of Jesus never fails.
Friends may forsake, but He avails.
Into His likeness, we are transformed.
In one accord, to Him we are conformed.
With God, forever be in tune.
Christ may return very soon.

At work or at play, with God, there is harmony.
"He is Lord!" That is our testimony.
From true believers, God's light does shine.
We walk and talk to the Lord divine.
Jesus is the light; He never fails.
When friends forsake, He still prevails.
With the Lord, we must keep in close touch.
He is coming soon; we love Him much.
Some Christian mentors already passed on to glory.
We must continue to spread the Gospel story.

Dedication to His Will

"For we are laborers together with God:
ye are God's husbandry,
ye are God's building."

I CORINTHIANS 3:9

We are devoted to our Master worker.
He's always at hand and won't be a shirker.
Lord, we will not insist on our own way.
Dominate our lives this day.
Whether the labor be easy or hard,
We vow to live by God's standard.
Be subject to God's divine plan.
When He calls, tell Him you can.
Our lives, to Him, we will consecrate,
On His work, we will concentrate.

With God, we are laborers together.
The harvest fields have souls to gather.
To be freed from danger,
Make God your manager.
On the Lord, our thoughts will be.
Our lives, in Him, bring victory.
We are faced with many tasks.
We fervently do what Jesus asks.
God's direction and guidance is imparted.
Our tasks for Christian service are wholehearted.

Disciple Yielded Vessels

"Notwithstanding in this rejoice not, that the spirits
are subject unto you; but rather rejoice, because your
names are written in heaven."

LUKE 10:20

True disciples will, His will obey.
They are fully yielded from day to day.
Christians need to be guided and restrained.
A yielded heart will be retrained.
Be not spiritually malicious.
A productive vessel is ambitious.
We want to know our duty in God's field.
Train and nurture fellow saints to yield.
We are compelled to be sanctified by grace.
We are fully committed, in each trial we face.

New Christians we must spiritually nourish.
When we are nurtured, we will flourish.
Continue to feed the soul
We have been saved and made whole.
God's sovereign grace is given free.
Discipleship is up to you and me.
Life goes on, and it is sometimes stressful.
Spiritual growth makes us spiritually successful.
We learn from the Word and can give it to others.
In this way we encourage our sisters and brothers.

Ready to Proclaim the Truth

"Preach the word; be instant in season; out of season;
reprove, rebuke, exhort with all
long-suffering and doctrine."

II TIMOTHY 4:2

No matter what the task we do today,
Let it be for God's glory, we pray.
Whatever the season, do your best.
Live for the moment through every test.
Be momentarily ready every day.
His abiding presence will lead the way.
Correct, rebuke and encourage.
Be patient and don't discourage.
Be sure to give careful instruction.
Carelessness leads to destruction.

The Bible is open; His Word we declare.
The gospel is preached everywhere.
On this we must be insistent:
Our faith in Christ is consistent.
Day by day, we watch and pray,
Listen intently to what He does say.
We live in the here and now.
The Lord must rule; He shows us how.
The Word of God we will proclaim.
Our prayers are entreated in Jesus' name.

The Ultimate Ascension

"And he said, 'Take now thy son, thine only son Isaac, whom thou lovest, and get thee into the land of Moriah; and offer him there for a burnt offering upon one of the mountains which I will tell thee of.'"

GENESIS 22:2

According to sincere belief, we will obey.
We will put our trust in Jesus; He is the Way.
God is the giver of whatever is good.
Count your blessings and do what you should.
To God, we will remain true.
Every day, He will renew.
Lord, may our faith be purified.
Through it You'll be glorified.
Our commitment is sometimes tested.
We will pass if, in Christ, we have rested.

Our God is one with purpose and life.
His presence avails in the midst of strife.
Religion does not save.
Christ, within, helps us behave.
When we know Him He meets our needs.
For whatever is right, the Spirit pleads.
Have faith in God and not in tradition.
His Word is truth; make no addition.
Listen to the voice of God and His Word alone.
Read the Word; heed to the truth; let it be known.

What Is Your Desire?

"And seekest thou great things for thyself?
Seek them not:"

JEREMIAH 45:5a

God loves to give us sweet surprises.
He gives more than one realizes.
O Lord, it is to You that we draw near.
We won't let selfishness interfere.
What we ask for should be in His will.
Each request, He will fulfill.
From God, we ask for admirable things,
I love You, Lord, the faithful sings.
Many blessings, the Lord does give.
Ask in His will; be co-operative.

Not for us,
But for Jesus.
Lord, help us to learn.
For Your glory, we yearn.
God knows the motives of our hearts.
Live for His glory; self-will departs.
Seek God's will and you will not be sorry.
Seek not mighty things for your own glory.
We wonder what it is that God wants us to have.
The gifts that He gives us are like healing salve.

Whatever He Wills, I'll Receive

"'I will bring evil upon all flesh,' saith the LORD: 'but thy life will I give unto thee for a prey in all places whither thou goest.'"

JEREMIAH 45:5b

Oh Lord, let us, in You, be hid.
From selfish interests, we will be rid.
When abiding in Christ, in Him we are trained.
Our lives for God are unrestrained.
When totally committed,
To Him, we have submitted.
The reward of obedience is the life He has prepared.
Nothing is better; it can't be compared.

Our minds are renewed with new ideals.
What is good and acceptable, appeals.
We share His vision.
He gives us provision.
Daily, on the Word, we are fed.
By the Spirit, we are led.
We will trust fully in Him, without disguise.
Our lives, hidden in Christ, are God's prize.
Trusting God brings delight and contentment.
A rich life in Christ gives us joy and not resentment.

The Pleasing Ease of Expectancy

"Beloved, now are we the sons of God, and it doth not yet appear what we shall be; but we know that, when He shall appear, we shall be like Him; for we shall see Him as He is."

I JOHN 3:2

Expect great things; God is on the throne.
He gives us surprises and calls us His own.
Of this one thing, we can be certain.
Between God and His children is no curtain.
Our life, in Him, is full of surprise events.
Rest upon His grace, as He hears our laments.
Look to this day with anticipation.
We're certain of God, with great expectation.
God has great plans for us.
This is what is required: Just trust Jesus.

Every morning, mercies are new.
They are waiting for me and for you.
To God, be rightly related.
Faith and purpose will be firmly stated.
God guides us one step at a time.
Walk forward with Him, each moment, sublime.
Our uncertainty about what is to come is gracious.
The promise of God, to us, is spacious.
We are children of God; this is a great revelation.
When conformed to His likeness we
have full salvation.

The Internal Cause of Love

"Charity suffereth long, and is kind; charity envieth not; charity vaunteth not itself, is not puffed up, doth not behave itself unseemly, seeketh not her own, is not easily provoked, thinketh no evil;"

I CORINTHIANS 13:4-5

Love, in God, is unconstrained.
In the Spirit, we are trained.
We need not tell of the good we will do.
The Spirit, within, will come shining through.
We love Him and He loves through us.
With joy and peace, He does renew us.
The love of God floods our hearts.
His very life, to us, He imparts.
Love is God's natural disposition.
We're safe in the Holy Spirit's supervision.

We want to show the love of God the most.
Rely on and yield to the Holy Ghost.
The Holy Spirit prompts us to share.
We spread God's love everywhere.
His love does please.
He carries it forth with ease.
Love that comes from God is perpetual.
That is because it is super-natural.
Love and obedience together are bound.
In born-again Christians, this nature is found.

May

For ye shall go out with joy, and be led forth
with peace: the mountains and the hills shall
break forth before you into singing, and all the
trees of the field shall clap their hands.
Isaiah 55:12

Clear Understanding, Not Excitement

"Therefore we are always confident, knowing that, whilst we are at home in the body, we are absent from the Lord:"

II CORINTHIANS 5:6

Let's not brag about our good deeds.
As we're led by faith, God supplies our needs.
Helpful acts are done without fanfare.
Here a little, there a little and everywhere.
Walk by spiritual insight, not emotion.
He's right there to accept our devotion.
We walk by faith and not by sight.
Fully trusting puts fears to flight.
Our standard is to do His will.
He is right there; He will fulfill.

Faith is a gift.
God gives a lift.
When God's way is sought,
Give Him your first thought.
Put tears and fears to flight.
Live by faith and not by sight.
By worldly ways and actions be not distracted.
Fix thoughts and eyes on Jesus; to Him be attracted.
Our desire must be put into action.
An accomplished task brings satisfaction.

Desire of Quiet Perseverance

"For the vision is yet for an appointed time, but at the end it shall speak, and not lie: though it tarry, wait for it; because it will surely come, it will not tarry."

HABAKKUK 2:3

Through each trial and testing, patience is wrought.
With our eyes on the Lord, fear is put to naught.
To do God's bidding is our submission.
Have patient endurance; His goal is our commission.
Look to the Lord and be inspired.
The vision before us has not expired.
We await the Lord's righteous intervention.
His appointed time will catch our attention.
To attain, we must reach.
The goal is before us; He will teach.

The kingdom of God is our goal.
Press on; be still, my soul.
Be patient; God is working.
Endure hard times; do not be shirking.
In the grasp of God, know that He gives us rest.
In Him, we rejoice; He gives what is best.
It takes awhile for a plant to bear fruit.
We will trust in the Lord; He alone is our pursuit.
The end result may be far beyond our reach.
Patience and fortitude is provided for each.

Essential Pleading

"Knowing that whatsoever good thing any man doeth,
the same shall he receive of the Lord, whether he be
bond or free."

EPHESIANS 6:8

Put Jesus first, others second, yourself last.
Intercede with joy, as you pray and fast.
It is the Lord we wish to exalt.
It's not our position to find fault.
With God, we will identify,
He, our lives, will sanctify.
Do not with sin and darkness flirt.
Pray continuously and be alert.
Pray in the Spirit on all occasions.
Minister love to all generations.

In constant communion,
What a blessed union.
Seek God's will in prayer.
All your burdens, He will bear.
We will not fear it.
We will pray in the Spirit.
Our identity with the Lord is necessary.
At the throne, we kneel and tarry.
As we pray in the Spirit, God's will is preferred.
We meet at His throne of grace; feast upon His Word.

Delegated Mediation

"Having therefore, brethren, boldness to enter into the
holiest by the blood of Jesus,""

HEBREWS 10:19

Sometimes our prayers become self-centered.
We need to be, by the Spirit, mentored.
We enter into the holiest by the blood Jesus shed.
Through our intercession, the gospel is spread.
Let us hold fast the hope we cherish.
Encourage each other; we will not perish.
We will not insist upon our own way.
We will intercede and trust Him each day.
Jesus shed His blood for us; we can be bold.
With Him, we identify; we will fit in His mold.

May our witness be faithful.
To the Lord, we are grateful.
To Christ we belong.
He makes us strong.
Of His presence, be always aware.
Of our own selfish interest, beware.
In each circumstance, may God be glorified.
We will not retreat for we are sanctified.
There is no greater entity,
Than to be in Christ's identity.

Divine Love Is What Matters

"For the time is come that judgment must begin at the
house of God: and if it first begin at us, what shall the
end be of them that obey not the gospel of God?"

I PETER 4:17

The Righteous Judge is on the throne.
He wants the Gospel to be known.
This is God's proclamation:
Jesus came to bring salvation.
The Gospel is God's Good News.
He yearns and waits for us to choose.
Salvation is God's thought.
What great things He has wrought.
We are so glad that, to Him, we belong.
When we are weak, He makes us strong.

God has taken all things into account.
Our selfish deeds will never count.
Our Lord is our Friend.
Our friendship will never end.
Christ has given full salvation.
His resurrected life, He does not ration.
When the truth is preached,
Lost souls are reached.
To exalt self is always appeasing.
We must do what is God-pleasing.

Freedom? Only in Christ!

"Stand fast therefore in the liberty wherewith Christ
hath made us free, and be not entangled again with
the yoke of bondage."

GALATIANS 5:1

Lord, we come on bended knee.
Only Christ will set us free.
To God's standard, we must conform.
He liberates; He does transform.
Do right and, to God, your soul commit.
Give Him glory as, to Him, you submit.
Believe the One whom the Bible reveals.
Go and make disciples, He appeals.
Jesus works within us to do what is right.
Stand fast in the liberty; walk in His light.

There is new life in Christ.
This has sufficed.
Christ has made us free.
We live in victory!
Religiosity will sometimes distort.
Jesus: Way, Truth, and Life; this is our retort.
He works on our conscience; His will is prominent.
We are liberated when Christ is predominant.
Faith is not built on a person's opinion
Hear the Word and believe that God has dominion.

Construction from God's Instruction

"For which of you, intending to build a tower, sitteth
not down first, and counteth the cost, whether he
have sufficient to finish it?"

LUKE 14:28

He laid down His life; have you counted the cost?
He gave His all to save the lost.
On the cross, He told us that it is finished.
His love and compassion has not diminished.
Our buildings, God will inspect.
So treat each building block with respect.
No other foundation can we lay.
Jesus Christ is the One; trust Him today.
To be a disciple, love Him the best.
Then we can enter into His rest.

Surrender all.
On His name, call.
Christ is our provision,
Trust not personal ambition.
Our own selfish plans can confuse and bewilder.
Only Almighty God is the right builder.
We have new hope because Christ is resurrected.
The goal of our faith is eternally protected.
By the ways and the things of this
world be not defiled.
It is through Christ that we are reconciled.

The Quiet Perseverance of Trusting

"Because thou hast kept the word of My patience, I also will keep thee from the hour of temptation, which shall come upon all the world, to try them that dwell upon the earth."

REVELATION 3:10

O Lord, we are safe in Your hands.
You are our God who understands.
Trust God with patience and you will endure.
Through trials and temptations, He makes us pure.
The goal is set before us and God takes aim.
Great things are accomplished in Jesus' name.
Oh Lord, help us not to run ahead.
Help us to know You first and then be led.
The Lord will keep us in the hour of trial.
We are safe in His arms; make no denial.

In faith, persevere.
The Lord we will revere.
On Him, your burdens cast.
Always remain steadfast.
Life is grand,
When He takes our hand.
Feed us, Lord, from Your Word.
It is there that Your voice is heard.
Stand strong in the Lord; in His name is power.
His Word within us is the faith endower.

Seize Firmly Without Straining

"Where there is no vision, the people perish,
but he that keepeth the law, happy is he."

PROVERBS 29:18

Don't lose sight of God's vision.
Be subject to His great commission.
We are morally inspired by the Spirit.
He speaks; we listen; be sure to hear it.
It may be good to have an ideal.
The law on our hearts has greater appeal.
God's high standard must be upheld.
Worldly ways will be repelled.
Be not, to the world, conformed.
By the Bible, be informed.

Rest in Him for He is just.
He does great things as we trust.
God has a purpose and a plan for our lives.
He sent His Son and our soul He revives.
We wonder what will really satisfy.
Only the Living Christ will sanctify.
God leads us on to higher ground.
We clasp His hand; we are safe and sound.
We pray and ask from God with expectation.
His abundant supply is no exaggeration.

The Direct Course of Getting Going

"Who are kept by the power of God through faith unto salvation ready to be revealed in the last time."

I PETER 1: 5

Lord, You have shown the way.
Help us to be quick to obey.
God will tell us what to do.
What we need is to follow through.
How can God, our problem make clear?
We will obey. His plan we will hear.
Resolve to do what is right and good.
When God speaks, do what you should.
Add to your faith Christian virtues.
Put the love of God into helpful use.

Our desire is to become involved.
To virtuous faith, we have resolved.
Lord, show us the way.
We will walk with You, day by day.
Your will we seek.
Listen; then speak.
Let your life be a holy example.
Christ is the message; He is ample.
To faith, we must virtue add.
In Christ, this virtue can be had.

Don't Stretch; Relax in Him

"And to godliness brotherly kindness; and to brotherly
kindness charity."

II PETER 1:7

Break up the fallow ground.
Divine love is safe and sound.
Above all else, the Lord we prefer.
To love others, to Him we refer.
The love we demonstrate is trained.
Yield to the Spirit; don't be constrained.
Be actively involved in Christian nurture.
By your faith, grow and mature.
To show forth love, put Jesus first.
In the Scriptures, be well-versed.

Love cannot be mustered up.
Each of us must drink His cup.
Have love and concern for everyone.
This is done through Christ, the Son.
We, in Christ, are found.
His divine love, in us, will abound.
Spiritual growth brings life with meaning.
We grow in grace, while fields we are gleaning.
The love God gives does not retire.
It is Jesus Christ that we admire.

Practice Becomes Natural

"For if these things be in you, and abound, they make
you that ye shall neither be barren nor unfruitful in the
knowledge of our Lord Jesus Christ."

II PETER 1:8

We have entered into His rest.
He helps us through the hardest test.
God's place is in every situation.
Speak His Word to each generation.
Our habits are lost in the Lord's life.
No more is our habit strife.
We rest in the confidence of His love.
We keep our thoughts on things above.
The qualities of Christ will abound.
Yielded hearts, in Him, are found.

We are not idle; we will bear fruit.
His will is our pursuit.
Through every test,
In Christ, we rest.
Godly action
Brings satisfaction.
Have spontaneous love.
He helps from above.
Do you have a bad habit? Lose it.
There is new life in Christ; choose it.

Practice Clear Understanding

"And therein I do exercise myself, to have always a conscience void of offence toward God, and toward men."

ACTS 24:16

To do God's will is our desire.
His perfect Way, He does inspire.
In the conscience, we are not offended.
His holy life, He has extended.
We will walk without offense.
His perfect will is our defense.
Is there any doubt that this is right?
Be sure what you do is not dark, but light.
God doesn't want us to be confused.
If there is a debate, it should be refused.

To God's guidance, we respond.
Of the Scriptures, we are fond.
Walk in the Spirit and be protected.
The slightest sin may be detected.
Our rule for morals is the Word of God.
Combat sinful ways and on His path trod.
A pure heart and a good conscience are the goal.
With divine love and grace, God makes us whole.
We want to make our calling and election sure.
Be effective and productive; the plans are pure.

Practice Being Happy

"Always bearing about in the body the dying of the Lord Jesus, that the life also of Jesus might be made manifest in our body."

II CORINTHIANS 4:10

Good habits express God's good grace.
God will exalt and not abase.
Disagreeable circumstances turn to delight.
His life is manifested; all is made right.
We are saved to show forth His life.
It's a life of sweetness and not of strife.
In salvation, we are given over to death.
Jesus' very life, He does bequeath.
Self-pity is no way to keep fit.
A child of the King, will the kingdom inherit.

May the life of Christ, in you, be manifest.
Live for His glory; He knows what is best.
When our faith in Christ is stable,
The Holy Spirit will enable.
We can still rejoice in the midst of trials.
Our Lord reigns; make no denials.
In a healthy soul, sin, God does restrict.
Keep yourself fit in the midst of daily conflict.
Let not the distractions of adversity get in your way.
Attraction we have for eternity in heaven is our stay.

Practice Manifesting His Glory

"The eyes of your understanding being enlightened;
that ye may know what is the hope of His calling, and
what the riches of the glory of His
inheritance in the saints,"

EPHESIANS 1:17-18

To give God glory is our goal.
He sanctifies and makes us whole.
We are children of God, in every occasion.
He helps us to boldly meet each situation.
We are delivered from the power of sin.
The victory is ours, with Christ within.
God saves and sanctifies; to Him we submit.
We exercise godliness; He makes us fit.
We are here to do God's will.
He supplies all and He will fulfill.

Through it all,
Don't let us fall.
When put through a test,
In God's arms just rest.
Give careful thought to your ways.
Cling to Jesus all your days.
The Lord is righteous and He loves what is just.
Take refuge in Him; this is a must.
We need to be productive and faith adoring.
Walk in the Spirit; God's will be exploring.

Practice of Acceptance of His Blessings

"Whereby are given unto us exceeding great and
precious promises: that by these ye might be
partakers of the divine nature, having escaped the
corruption that is in the world through lust."

II PETER 1:4

Our Heavenly Father is wealthy.
He supplies our needs and keeps us healthy.
God's nature is to give.
In His grace, we live.
Of His Word, we do partake.
We do what we do, for Jesus' sake.
In Christ Jesus, we have God's abundance.
The Words He speaks need no redundance
When facing a mountain height,
Let God be foremost in your sight.

We will make no denies.
The Lord supplies!
In self-pity, we are fretful and sad.
God's divine Nature makes us glad.
Take selfish interest off the throne.
We are rich in Christ; make this known.
God's grace is sufficient;
do not grumble and complain.
Self-pity is absent when, in Christ, we remain.
No longer rest in human appetites and desires.
Feast on the Word of God; this is what inspires.

Seated in the Heavenlies

"And it came to pass, while He blessed
them, He was parted from them and
carried up into heaven."

LUKE 24:51

Our Lord entered heaven and opens the door.
His attributes He gives; could we ask for more?
We enter into God's life through the blood.
The door is the cross, and with the Spirit He'll flood.
His life, presence and power He imparts.
We are enriched, when He enters our hearts.
The Son of man is the King of kings.
Only He, full salvation brings.
There is no glory without the cross.
Our trust in Him will mean no loss.

Heaven is our goal.
He cleansed from sin and made us whole.
Jesus meets us in our need.
At the throne, He will intercede.
Jesus, the Lamb of God, was slain.
Through Him, salvation, we obtain.
The Son of God is seated on His throne.
How marvelous it is that He calls us as His own.
God has promised His blessing on those who receive.
Look to Jesus; love and obey Him;
to His mercy, cleave.

Watchful Naturalness

"Behold the fowls of the air: for they sow not, neither
do they reap, nor gather into barns; yet your heavenly
Father feedeth them. Are ye not much better than
they? And why take ye thought for raiment? Consider
the lilies of the field, how they grow; they toil not,
neither do they spin:"

MATTHEW 6 26, 28

Trust in Him; He will see you through.
He is there to strengthen and renew.
Consider the lilies; they neither toil nor spin.
Why worry or fret, when He lives within?
Out of you will flow rivers of living water.
Jesus brings our petitions to the Father.
We need not muster up love and compassion.
In Him it comes naturally; that is His fashion.
God has promised to supply what is needed.
Just yield to Him; to His will be heeded.

Do not worry or be filled with remorse.
Count your blessings and consider the source.
Remember: God is the provider; He supplies.
You are precious in His eyes.
To live a life of victory,
Just trust. He will free.
To Jesus Christ, be rightly related.
Your worries and cares won't be widely inflated.
Live each day in a simple manner.
Remember that God is our greatest day planner.

Mangled, But Not Strangled

"Who shall separate us from the love of Christ? shall tribulation, or distress, or persecution, or famine, or nakedness, or peril, or sword?"

ROMANS 8:35

In the midst of trials, be not dismayed.
We are more than conquerors; we are heaven made.
From God, we won't be separated.
Jesus Christ has liberated.
God sees and helps through troubled times.
Jesus is the best of all paradigms.
He walks with us through the valley.
Continue onward and upward; don't dally.
God is love; that is a fact.
His love affects the way we act.

In the Lord, we are secure.
He answers prayer and makes us pure.
In the midst of our distress,
God will straighten out our mess.
Forget what is behind.
Heaven's blessings you will find.
God extends His love and blessings everywhere.
In the midst of turmoil, He says I care.
No longer with worldly ways are we enamored
We advance toward the goal and trust in the Lord.

The Region of Actuality

"In your patience possess ye your souls."

LUKE 21:19

In Christ, new life is found.
Be no longer, by satan, bound.
The Lord bestows peace and contentment.
Open your heart; have no resentment.
Emotions can be restrained.
Patience, in the Spirit, is attained.
In persevering faith stand firm.
He is able and that is what we affirm.
Victory is gained when we persevere.
Doubt and failure will disappear.

Speak the Word of the Lord.
It can be your sword.
We go through the door;
The Lord, we implore.
We must go; we want more.
New life, in Christ, we will explore.
We have found the door of life; Christ is within.
With steadfastness and patience, we will win.
Our souls He does make whole;
we love Him the most.
We belong to Him; He is our Head and our Host.

Sacred Motives of Loyalty to God

"But seek ye first the kingdom of God, and His righteousness; and all these things shall be added unto you."

MATTHEW 6:33

We will seek Your kingdom first.
For Your righteousness we thirst.
On the Lord, we will concentrate.
Our lives, our all, we will consecrate.
May faith be your divine reasoning.
May salt be your seasoning.
In thoughts and deeds, Christ is number one.
It is then that we show love to everyone.
In God's kingdom, His wisdom is in action.
Righteousness rules in spiritual satisfaction.

Let God be your mission.
It is a Christian's ambition.
Self-glory is wrong.
To Christ, we belong.
Seek God's authority and excellence
This will lead to a godly eloquence.
Seek the Lord and don't forsake His power.
Abandon selfish ways and reach out to Him this hour.
We let God's prevalent plan be our first concern.
Trust fully in Him, and from the Word of God learn.

Be One with the Father and the Son

"That they all may be one; as thou, Father, art in Me,
and I in Thee, that they also may be one in us; that
the world may believe that thou hast sent Me."

JOHN 17: 21

Jesus prayed that we be one.
Be one with the Father and one with the Son.
The Triune God is on the throne.
He claims His disciples as His own.
We pray to the Father and ask for His will.
Always trust in Him; He will fulfill.
Love not the world; read the Word; reach the lost.
In humility, bear the cross at any cost.
Keep the unity through the bond of peace.
When we walk together, contention will cease.

In God's family, we are united.
Share the love; in His kingdom we are delighted.
Some times may be hard to bear.
Just remember; God is there.
Are you feeling bewildered and alone?
May God's loving care be known.
Through each trial we become either better or bitter.
Draw near to God; be a "getter" and not a "quitter."
True unity of believers assures us of God's glory.
With heart and purpose, our lives are exclamatory.

Watchful Treachery

"Therefore I say unto you, Take no thought for your
life, what ye shall eat, or what ye shall drink; nor yet
for your body, what ye shall put on. Is not the life
more than meat, and the body than raiment?"

MATTHEW 6:25

God must have first place.
Only then, can we win the race.
Make cares and worry obliteration.
God is our first consideration.
Do not be fretful or confuse.
Trust in His care and never abuse.
God has promised to supply our needs.
Consider Him first, as the Spirit leads.
When, to the Lord, we are fully yielded.
From all evil we will be shielded.

Our lives won't be full of hurry and scurry.
The Word of God says we should not worry.
Believe and trust.
Faith is a must.
We want to do what God has planned;
this we consider.
Lord, help each one of us to be a loyal submitter.
With worldly cares do not hook up.
Just continue to trust the Lord and look up!
Earthly cares are heavy; they lead to fearful emotion.
Love and devotion is the way we have chosen.

Great Satisfaction in Hopelessness

"And when I saw Him, I fell at His feet as dead. And He laid His right hand upon me, saying unto me. 'Fear not; I am the first and the last:'"

REVELATION 1:17

In the midst of discouragement,
God gives loving encouragement.
How majestic is His presence.
His nearness is sweet essence.
When we are sad and in despair,
He lifts us up and says He does care.
Some things are hard to understand.
God tell us not to fear; He then extends His hand.
How good it is to feel Jesus' touch.
He comes; we know He loves us much.

God's hand is gracious.
His love is spacious.
We live in God's grace.
We sing His praise.
The mercy of God delights us.
When things go wrong, He rights us.
God makes all things possible; faith is essential.
To receive, believe; delight is consequential.
Marvelous resources our Lord has planned.
He gives again and again; on His Word we stand.

The Critical Exam of Selfishness

"Is not the whole land before thee? Separate thyself,
I pray thee, from me: if thou wilt take the left hand,
then I will go to the right; or if thou depart to the right
hand, then I will go to the left."

GENESIS 13:9

There is a right way; we will let God choose.
When He makes decisions, we will not lose.
To satisfy self is not always right.
Want what God wants; He knows your plight.
This is how we pass the test:
Choose faith in God; enter His rest.
Let the Lord guide you on your path.
He will keep you from sin and wrath.
Good is the enemy of best.
The Lord will show us the way; that is our request.

What I want may not be right.
I'll follow God with all my might.
Upon the Lord, we pray and wait.
He will make our pathway straight.
We are faced with a selection.
Wait on the Lord; take His direction.
We wonder which way is right.
On God's path, we walk in the light.
Sometimes we are tempted to go astray.
We must trust the Lord's leading as we pray.

Consider His Teachings

"Pray without ceasing."

I THESSALONIANS 5:17

Prayer is the Christian's life-giving breath.
All of God's promises, He does bequeath.
Moment by moment, we can breathe out a prayer.
The Lord is present everywhere.
Pray without ceasing.
Your faith is increasing.
Pray continually for the Father's grace and blessing.
At the same time, faith, we are confessing.
Let prayer never cease.
God grants us His peace.

Prayer determines how we walk.
It affects what we do and how we talk.
We want to do and say what we ought.
Constantly pray, as Jesus taught.
In everything, give thanks and pray.
Believe; God's answer is on the way.
Prayer is essential in the life of every saint.
It helps us to proceed, to be strong and not faint.
For what God has provided, be no longer defiant.
Be not self centered, but on Christ be reliant.

The Vitality of Spiritual Quickening

"And, behold, I send the promise of My Father upon you: but tarry ye in the city of Jerusalem, until ye be endued with power from on high."

LUKE 24:49

He has endued us with His power.
The Holy Spirit avails this hour.
The Lord ascended and sent the Spirit.
He quickens lives; we need not fear it.
God's providence always avails.
Be spiritually fit; He never fails.
We glory in the presence of His grace.
The Spirit is within; each trial we can face.
As we wait upon Him, strength is renewed.
With His power, we are endued.

We need not strive.
Christ is alive!
This very hour,
The Spirit gives power.
The Lord has made us stable.
He does constantly enable.
Love for the Lord increases as, on Him, we ponder.
We're endued with the Holy Spirit and will not wander.
He leads and guides; the risen Christ is evident.
God's constant mercy and grace is provident.

Complete Trust in His Promises

"Hitherto have ye asked nothing in My name: ask,
and ye shall receive, that your joy may be full."

JOHN 16:23

Lord, we want to live with Your purpose in mind.
To Your life and, to Your way, we are inclined.
Life, in Christ, is a perfect union.
We live with Him in sweet communion.
On His resurrection life, we can rely.
He continues to supply.
Lord, Your grace is with us still.
We will walk within Your will.
Whatever we ask, in Jesus name,
We will receive; His love is our aim.

In His life, we are secure.
The whys are gone and we endure.
On His resurrection life we rely.
His living presence, don't deny.
Step by step, our Savior leads.
He supplies us with our needs.
On new life, in Christ, we can depend.
What a perfect union; it is secure and without end.
Life in the Spirit is a life of security.
He endues His power; we live in Christ's purity.

Peaceful Kinship

"At that day ye shall ask in My name: and I say not unto you, that 'I will pray the Father for you: For the Father Himself loveth you, because ye have loved Me, and have believed that I came out from God."

JOHN 16:26- 27

In Christ, we are at one in heart and mind.
A more loving relationship we will never find.
In heavenly places, God gives pure advice.
We are rightly related and His message is precise.
Ask of the Father, in Jesus' Name.
His will and purpose will be our aim.
Our union with our Lord is complete.
We are confident, as each trial we meet.
He lifts us up into heavenly places.
We're made complete within His graces.

When there is a job to do,
The loving Lord enables you.
As soldiers, we will fight.
He always helps us to do what is right.
To the Father, we have access.
The name of Jesus, we will profess.
Do not hesitate to move ahead.
Have no fear; trust God, instead.
God's greatness is shown; follow His commands.
Go forth to achieve the mission; He understands.

Go Forth with Joy

"And another also said, 'Lord, I will follow Thee; but let me first go bid them farewell, which are at home at my house.'"

LUKE 9:61

We are determined to trust Him wholly.
We have unbroken fellowship with the Lord most holy.
God leads and guides into hard ventures.
We plunge right into the bold adventures.
We will trust God with all our heart.
From His instruction we will not depart.
Lord, we will follow; in You we trust.
A leap of faith is always a must.
When plowing a furrow, don't look back.
The Lord will lead; you'll have no lack.

On the Word, we meditate.
Obey, and do not hesitate.
God tells us to go.
Let us not say no.
When God calls you, don't send someone else.
Obey His voice where He compels.
God gives us orders; we are selected.
We must follow as He has directed.
We don't see the future; the Lord has a plan.
He shines the light, the pathway to span.

Jehovah is Number One

"But Jesus did not commit Himself unto them,
because He knew all men, and needed not that any
should testify of man: for He knew what was in man."

JOHN 2:24-25

Man has no righteousness in self alone.
Only Christ's sacrifice of blood does atone.
Lord, we desire to do Your will.
We will trust in You and You will fulfill.
Always, in everything, put God first.
With living water, He'll quench your thirst.
Jesus knows what is in the heart of man.
God's will should be in our master plan.
We are fully trusting in God's grace.
It is expedient that He have first place.

Christ is our pure perfection.
Always give Him first affection.
With Him, we are co-workers.
By His grace, we will not be shirkers.
Though this world is filled with sorrow and strife,
May the joy of the Lord permeate each life.
Trust in the Lord; give Christ first place.
The presence of God we will forever embrace.
May God's glory shine through us;
He does what is best.
May the Son of God in our lives be made manifest.

June

Behold, He cometh with clouds; and every eye shall see Him, and they also which pierced Him: and all kindreds of the earth shall wail because of Him. Even so, Amen.
Revelation 1:7

Astounding Inquiry

"And He said unto me, 'Son of man, can these bones
live?' And I answered, 'O Lord God, thou knowest.'"

EZEKIEL 37:3

God's grace accomplishes a lot.
Do not worry or fret, when His will is sought.
With God, we are fellow workers.
When trusting Him, we will be faith perkers.
A sinner can be turned into a saint.
The Holy Spirit brings restraint.
Breathe on us, Lord, the breath of life.
Restore and deliver us from strife.
The dry bones will be again restored.
Faith is renewed as we call on the Lord.

We go in the fields together.
Yoked with God, could be no better.
In Him, the Christian lives.
We worship; He gives.
Work with God consistently.
His grace is sufficient, insistently.
We want to know what to do, so we inquire.
Each step of the way, God will inspire.
God can straighten lives that appear to be twisted.
It happens when the Holy Spirit is no longer resisted.

Are You Frequently Visited By Fear?

"What man is he that feareth the LORD? him shall
He teach in the way that He shall choose."

PSALMS 25:12

Don't let self get in the way.
Trust in the Lord; do not dismay.
Believe and let not worry even enter.
In every thought, the Lord is at the center.
To fear the Lord is wise.
An abiding saint needs no disguise.
The enemy is aiming at destruction.
In the midst of trials, God gives His instruction.
God, in His wisdom, guides each believer.
His paths are righteous to each receiver.

God will appoint.
He will not disappoint.
In Him, there is pleasure.
He gives love and joy beyond measure.
What greater happiness could be possessed?
In the Lord, we have joy and we are blessed.
Souls for the kingdom, we are inviting.
To know and love the Lord is so exciting!
In God's harbor we are safe and protected.
God permits incidents; His will is detected.

He Knows Even Our Thoughts

"The secret of the LORD is with them that fear Him;
and He will show them His covenant."

PSALMS 25:14

When doing His will, the word is go.
The smallest detail, the Lord does know.
Secret joys are shared with a friend.
God knows everything, from beginning to end.
The world compels us to step out.
Stay at home, when there is doubt.
With God's purposes, stay in touch.
We're saved and sanctified; He loves us much.
Fear the Lord and in Him confide.
Shun evil; in His love abide.

Little secret joys we share.
God loves and blesses everywhere.
With sin, do not flirt.
If it is doubtful it is dirt.
Do the things you will not regret.
The Lord, to you, reveals His secret.
In the midst of trials, the Lord gives joy and strength.
His will is done; our confidence extends full length.
In Christ, there is much joy and satisfaction.
He leads and guides us into action.

At No Time, Will God Disappoint

"Let your conversation be without covetousness; and be content with such things as ye have: for He hath said, 'I will never leave thee, nor forsake thee.'"

HEBREWS 13:5

God's love and mercy does avail.
He will not forsake, nor will He fail.
God tells us that He is the Lord that heals us.
We believe; He has set us free in Jesus.
With the Lord as our Helper, we need not fear.
When He speaks, we need to hear.
The Lord will never leave, nor forsake.
Of His grace, we can partake.
God leads us on day by day.
We trust in Him; He leads the way.

He will not abandon; we will not deny.
His blessings we grasp; on Him, we rely.
Day by day, God does appoint.
With His power, He will anoint.
Each day the Lord does assure and invite.
Happy are those who, in Him, delight.
God's Word we will embrace.
He enables us, each trial to face.
Moment by moment, in Him we are content.
Time spent with Him is time is well spent.

God's Word is Confirmed

"Let your conversation be without covetousness; and be content with such things as ye have: For He hath said, 'I will never leave thee, nor forsake thee.' So that we may boldly say, 'The Lord is my Helper, and I will not fear what man shall do unto me.'"

HEBREWS 13:6

God's Word is truth; we will believe it.
He gives and gives and we receive it.
The Lord is my Helper; we will not fear.
When He speaks, His voice we will hear.
God has promised: He will never leave.
His grace abounds and we achieve.
He is ever present and never fails.
The power of God still prevails.
The Lord is our strength; we will not be afraid.
That is confirmed in the covenant, long ago made.

God is forever near.
Rightly, we should never fear.
In Him, we are assured.
We trust in God's Word.
To God be reconciled, live in peace.
From fear and worry, He brings release.
This is what we will report:
The Almighty God brings peace and comfort.
Greed and immorality are partners in offense.
Much wealth may have a harmful consequence.

A Sanctified Workout with Jesus

"Wherefore, my beloved, as ye have always obeyed,
not as in my presence only, but now much more in my
absence, work out your own salvation with
fear and trembling."

PHILIPPIANS 2:12

Our desire is to do what God has willed.
May we be with the Holy Spirit filled.
In Christ, the will and conscience agree.
What needs to be done, may He do through
you and me.
Our almighty God helps us to see.
We will walk in His integrity.
Redemption, through Christ, is a divine treasure.
To work within us is His pleasure.
The fear of the Lord is pure and cleansing.
His very life, He is dispensing.

Wait on Him with expectation.
We are renewed with anticipation.
Do not fear and fret and pout.
Our loving God will work it out.
Be not hindered by the world's distraction.
Put what you have learned into action.
We work out to be spiritually fit.
God works, as to Him, we commit.
Evil thoughts and actions will be destroyed.
What God wants us to do, we will not avoid.

Indifference is Unfruitful

"And whatsoever ye shall ask in My Name, that will I do, that the Father may be glorified in the Son."

JOHN 14:13

To bring forth fruit, we intercede.
He supplies our every need.
Jesus Christ is at the center.
It is He that is our mentor.
In consecration, don't be slack.
In Jesus Christ, there is no lack.
What we ask for, He will do.
He has atoned; He does renew.
The ministry of intercession is hidden.
God knows our thoughts and gives what is bidden.

Hide God's Word in the heart,
From the precepts don't depart.
We are, in the Lord, confiding.
He is constantly abiding.
To keep upon a steady course,
Remember, Jesus is the source.
The Holy Spirit's power is demonstrated.
The gifts He gives are allocated.
The Word of God is the dominating factor.
He is Lord; could there be a better benefactor?

Will You Refuse or Excuse or Enthuse?

"If ye know these things,
happy are ye if ye do them."

JOHN 13:17

We must launch out in waters deep.
The waves may be high, but God does not sleep.
Live and learn and for His fullness yearn.
When you really know Him, He will help you discern.
Obey and He, your heart, will gladden.
Regressive action will stunt and sadden.
To this world's system, do not conform.
Adhere to God's standard; He will transform.
From the Word of the Lord, we are inspired.
We will walk in the Spirit; be alert and not tired.

Launch out into deep waters.
Be an obedient sons and daughters.
To learn more,
We must leave the shore.
Be not hindered by the world's distraction.
Put what you have learned into action.
What God tells us from His Word, we will share.
Help us, Lord, to publish Your message everywhere.
Read the Word and obey; by the Holy Spirit, be led.
Move forward; the Lord lights the pathway ahead.

Immediately Following the Need, Pray

"For every one that asketh, receiveth; and he that
seeketh, findeth; and to him that knocketh,
it shall be opened."

LUKE 11:10

Learn to ask early; ask of the Lord what to do.
He has set free and He lives in you.
Through the Holy Spirit, we make our appeal.
He is the One who makes Christ's love real.
If there is any lack, just ask.
God will fulfill for every task.
Ask boldly of Him and He will give.
For His purpose, we will live.
When we ask of God, according to His will,
He is ready and willing our desires to fulfill.

When we sincerely ask,
He fits us for each task.
May knowing God be an eager desire.
Walk constantly with our grace supplier.
May our zeal be renewed and vision refreshed.
May we walk in the light, not in darkness enmeshed.
We are servants of Christ; make no mistake.
Never serve other gods or the Lord forsake.
Ask the Lord for guidance and seek His support.
His purpose and passion, yields a good report.

Ask and Expect

"And I say unto you, Ask, and it shall be given you;
seek, and ye shall find; knock, and it shall be opened
unto you."

LUKE 11:9

Not self-glory, but the Lord, we seek.
His Spirit is strong; the flesh is weak.
Satisfying self is not fulfilling.
God must be first to supply; He is willing.
Love the Lord with all your heart, soul and mind.
When you seek Him, fully, you will find.
When thirsty, come to His Living Waters and drink.
The Lord will give much more than you think.
Humble yourself and of God implore.
He is willing and able to give much more.

What we ask for humbly and in His will we will get.
He hears our pleas and won't forget.
Ask, seek, and knock; proceed in that order.
Give generously, and don't be a hoarder.
Seek earnestly for what you desire.
He hears your prayer; He's not a denier.
Our needs are met, when we seek God and knock.
He answers our prayer; He cares for His flock.
We will ask in prayer; the request will be granted.
As we abide in Christ, our faith is firmly planted.

How to Arrive

"Come unto me, all ye that labor and are heavy laden,
and I will give you rest."

MATTHEW 11:28

When we enter into His rest,
Know there is comfort; He knows what is best.
Jesus still says "Come unto Me."
What He wants, we want; He has set free!
Our lives, with Jesus, are in one accord.
Just come to Him, for He is Lord.
Life in Him is satisfying.
He does it all, we are testifying.
The song and the saint come together.
Have joy in your heart in any weather.

What a fascinating choice!
In Him, we can rejoice.
Come to Jesus with courage and zest.
He will always give the best.
God invites us to come to Him; that's His plea.
He has provided victory.
Come into His presence; turn away from sin.
In Him is full joy; in Him, we win.
Christ's invitation is to a divine union.
We are eternally blessed with sweet communion.

Arriving to Stay

"Then Jesus turned, and saw them following, and
saith unto them, 'What seek ye?' They said unto Him,
'Rabbi, (Master) where dwellest Thou?' He saith unto
them, 'Come and see.' They came and saw where
He dwelt, and abode with Him that day; for it was
about the tenth hour."

JOHN 1:38, 39

Take from us the foolish name of pride.
We come to You, Lord, and in You we abide.
We will put our own interests on a shelf.
We are alive to God and dead to self.
We abide in Him in all conditions.
He's always present, with no omissions.
Jesus is our all-in-all.
He is within; we will not fall.
To walk in the flesh, we are sure to fail.
Walk in the Spirit; His power does avail.

With our living Lord, we are acquainted.
Each believer, He has sainted.
With our eyes fixed on Jesus,
His presence will please us.
The Messiah is Jesus, the expected Savior.
His grace and mercy affect our behavior.
May selfishness and pride be what we erase.
We love the Lord and we live in His grace.
Jesus is our all in all, we'll trust Him and not fall.
Self-interest is gone; the cross is standing tall.

Obtaining That Place

"And Jesus said unto them, 'Come ye after Me, and I
will make you to become fishers of men.'"

MARK 1:17

Lord, make our lives a sacrifice.
Only You are all-knowing and all-loving, we realize.
With the Lord, always strive to agree.
Abandoned to Him, we are set free.
All to Him, we will surrender.
He is our strong fortress and defender.
God is in charge in all circumstances.
All is well when He enhances.
He who wins souls is wise.
Conform to convictions; don't compromise.

Our lives, in Christ, are a testament.
To come to Him, is our intent.
He tells us to come and we will follow.
On murky paths, we do not wallow.
When we have problems; we plead.
Our Lord Jesus will lead.
How do we get there?
Follow Him; be aware.
Our lives, to Christ, we will abandon.
It is finished; it is done.

Forever Forward

"Abide in Me, and I in you. As the branch cannot bear
fruit of itself, except it abide in the vine; no more can
ye, except ye abide in Me."

JOHN 15:4

Our Lord is aware of every thought.
Evil deeds are put to naught.
Jesus abides in every situation.
We will rest in Him; that is our obligation.
Be at one with Christ and in one accord.
We will trust fully in the Lord.
He guides our actions as, in Him, we remain.
To trust in self is to trust in vain.
Keep God's Word continually in heart and mind.
No greater reference will you ever find.

In Him, we are at home.
We are together, wherever we roam.
He is with us, always.
His blessings fill our days.
A hunger for the Lord is healthy.
Feast on the Word and be spiritually wealthy.
When we follow Christ, His will we obey.
He wants us to trust Him; His life down He lay.
Walk in the good way and find rest in your soul.
The mind of Christ blesses and makes you whole.

There is Much More in Jesus

"And beside this, giving all diligence, add to your faith
virtue; and to virtue knowledge;"

II PETER 1:5

God provides His nature, divine.
I can call His holiness mine.
Habits are changed, because life is new.
In each task, let His light shine through.
God's power is in every detail.
His mercy and grace do prevail.
Add to your faith goodness,
knowledge and self-control.
Add perseverance, kindness, and love and be whole.
Be actively involved in Christian growing.
Accept the grace that He keeps bestowing.

Don't wait for applause.
Make Jesus your cause.
Perseverance proves faith to be real.
We press on towards the goal; that is our appeal.
We must not be sad and moody.
To proclaim Christ, is our divine duty.
Don't wait for approval to be expressed.
It is only by God's grace that we have impressed.
Even if the audience is only one,
Remember the goal: lift up the Son.

Will This Bring Honor, or Disgrace?

"Greater love hath no man than this, that a man lay down his life for his friends. Henceforth I call you not servants; for the servant knoweth not what his lord doeth; but I have called you friends; for all things that I have heard of my Father I have made known unto you."

JOHN 15:13, 15

Jesus, our Friend, laid down His life.
We can do the same in the midst of strife.
Walk in the light of the moment.
Be under God's management.
Jesus has called us friends.
His grace and mercy never ends.
The way of the world has been perverted.
Give God your life, that many be converted.
Our desire for earthly gain is dead,
When we will live for His glory instead.

Make Christ the center of every thought.
He is our Savior; we will do what we ought.
Not I, but Christ, in every activity.
The result will exalt His Divinity.
We will not worry and frown;
Our lives, we will lay down.
New life, in Christ, is a life that is exchanged.
It is no longer I who lives; it is all rearranged.
Live moral lives; God's honor is at stake.
How we choose to walk will either make or break.

Not a Fault-Finding Attitude of Mind

"Judge not, that ye be not judged."

MATTHEW 7: 1

Who are we to criticize?
Each saint is precious in His eyes.
The Holy Spirit finds the fault.
It is our duty, the Lord to exalt.
Only the Lord can rightly judge.
When we criticize, the Spirit will nudge.
Don't look for flaws in others and ignore your own.
There may be reasons that, to you, are not known.
By grace, alone, are we made whole.
Let the Holy Spirit take control.

Do not point fingers at those who do wrong.
Praise the Lord; exalt Him with song.
Emphasize in others what is good.
Walk on, and do what you know you should.
We see bad things in other's blunders.
Their small mistakes resound like thunders.
Throw off what hinders your walk with the Lord.
Look not back; in Christ, faith is restored.
We will not judge others or use a measuring rod.
To expose weakness, we neglect the grace of God.

Obstruction Need Not Be Destruction

"And he said, 'Come,' And when Peter was come down out of the ship, he walked on the water, to go to Jesus. But when he saw the wind boisterous, he was afraid; and beginning to sink, he cried, saying, 'Lord, save me.'"

MATTHEW 14: 29, 30

God will give divine instruction.
Keep your eyes on Him, not the obstruction.
Ignore the wind and storm and waves.
Put your trust in Him; Jesus saves!
Trust in Jesus and do not doubt.
Follow His path, as He calls you out.
On Him, rely completely now.
His attributes, He does endow.
Jesus tells us to take courage and not be afraid.
Each circumstance has been obeyed.

If we look at the waves, we lose our nerve.
Look to Jesus; from His path, don't swerve.
Fear not the wind on the sea.
Always know Jesus saves and sets free.
When in distress,
Faith, we confess.
We will not fall for Satan's tricks.
On the Lord, our eyes we fix.
Even if the wind is boisterous, we will not fear.
God reaches forth His hand; He is forever near.

Attending to Emotional Support

"He saith to him again the second time, 'Simon, son
of Jonas, lovest thou Me?' He saith unto Him, 'Yea,
Lord; thou knowest that I love Thee.' He saith unto
him, 'Feed My sheep.'"

JOHN 21:16

Jesus is our Friend, indeed.
We are devoted to Him, and not to creed.
We want to know Him more each day.
We want to hear His truth and walk in His way.
We will be His disciples; to Him we are devoted.
Love and compassion are not outmoded.
We need guidance, correction and protection.
Each day, walk in His direction.
We need to feed constantly on the Word.
The Shepherd calls; His voice is heard.

To Jesus Christ, be devoted.
The Father's will is then promoted.
Faith is belief and trust.
To do His will is a must.
May devotion to God be our passion.
Love others and have compassion.
We live in joy; our faith is evident.
Our position is affirmed; God's Word is provident.
We must always give credit where credit is due.
The joy of the Lord is strength in me and in you.

In Christ, it is Done

"And the LORD turned the captivity of Job, when he prayed for his friends: also the LORD gave Job twice as much as he had before."

JOB 42:10

Oh Lord, we will intercede.
We will help a friend in need.
We accept the finished work.
We are saved; God does not shirk.
On the cross the work was done.
Simply trust in Christ, the Son.
Lord, we pray for those we meet.
Your atonement is for all, not just the elite.
The Lord Jesus Christ is our example.
By His atonement, He is ample.

When our friends have a need,
We are called upon to intercede.
Our losses are restored;
Bring others to the Lord.
Our answers to prayer are sometimes delayed.
The Lord may make changes to
what we have prayed.
As saved souls, what is most necessary?
Prayers for our friends are intercessory.
Our prayers are constant; we never give up.
It is a vital part of a Christian's makeup.

Supplying the Needs of the Saints

"But ye are a chosen generation, a royal priesthood,
and holy nation, a peculiar people; that ye should
show forth the praises of Him who hath called you out
of darkness into His marvelous light:"

I PETER 2:9

As royal priests, we've been reconciled.
Jesus is holy and not defiled.
We are at one, with Christ, because He lives.
We pray; we trust; He gives!
In Christ Jesus, take delight.
Saints are precious in His sight.
We will profess the gospel to His glory and praise.
In Christ Jesus, alone, we take our place.
His royal priesthood does amaze.
On Christ's merit, His Word we raise.

We can intercede in prayer.
The love of Jesus, we will share.
Heaven is of royal domain.
In Christ, an inheritance we obtain.
To the Lord Jesus Christ, we will be true.
How much He loves me and you.
Our position, in Christ, is very significant.
It is a ministry that is most magnificent.
To be one with Christ is our faithful ambition.
We are secure in this God ordained mission.

Resolved to His Purpose

"Judge not, that ye be not judged. For with what judgment ye judge, ye shall be judged; and with what measure ye mete, it shall be measured to you again."

MATTHEW 7:1-2

From God's path, we will not turn.
In humility, let us learn.
What will be our contribution?
We'll be given back in retribution.
Have we a right to judge another person?
In criticizing, our own faults may worsen.
Judging others can spell disaster.
Just trust Jesus as your Lord and Master.
When we judge others, we point out defects.
Our judgmental statements have ill-effects.

We must encourage,
And not discourage.
Look not for mistakes in others.
Judge not sisters and brothers.
Treat each one kindly and don't condemn.
It is God who wears the diadem.
It is only by grace that our sinful nature is changed.
The life that we have lived is, by Christ, exchanged.
Many people have made many errors.
Repentance cleanses and releases from terrors.

Deep Sorrow

"He is despised and rejected of men; a man of
sorrows, and acquainted with grief: and we hid as it
were our faces from Him; He was despised, and we
esteemed Him not."

ISAIAH 53:3

Sin, on earth, is running rampant, full-sway.
Accept Jesus, who washes the sin away.
With grief, our Lord is acquainted.
Choose God, not sin, for it is tainted.
We must choose between God and sin.
In Christ, alone, we're cleansed within.
There will be trials and troubles in each tomorrow.
But Christ will see us through each sorrow.
There is sin and there is Christ; we must choose.
In Christ we win; in sin, we lose.

New life is our explanation.
In Christ, we are a new creation.
Sin brings sorrow to our hearts.
Come to Jesus; His life, He imparts.
Sinfulness or godliness? Which way will you live?
Follow Jesus; His life, He does give.
We are selected and we live a life of joy with Him.
We are given new life and our lights will not dim.
In Christ, we are triumphantly identified.
Victory over sin belongs to the sanctified.

Resigned to the Fact of Transgression

"When I was daily with you in the temple, ye stretched forth no hands against Me: but this is your hour, and the power of darkness."

LUKE 22:53

Sin may lurk around a corner.
The light of the Word is our fair warrior.
Be not deceived by self nobility.
Jesus alone, gives grace ability.
Sin does exist: that is a fact.
Christ avails; He will counteract.
Live by the truth; come into His light.
Sin and darkness will be put to flight.
Sin is a threat; that's the Lord's opinion.
In Christ, sin no longer has dominion.

How can we be safe and free?
Look to the Lord, constantly.
Sin and evil will surely annoy.
It is the Lord and His goodness that we enjoy.
It is right there: the temptation to sin.
Victory is ahead, when Christ lives within.
Face the fact of sin; be virtuous and pure.
Refuse all evil; God's grace is sure.
Evil is prevalent, but God's grace is much stronger.
We need not wallow in worldly ways any longer.

His Cause in the Midst of Grief

"Now is my soul troubled: and what shall I say?
'Father, save Me from this hour: but for this cause
came I unto this hour. Father, glorify thy name.' Then
came there a voice from heaven, saying, 'I have both
glorified it, and will glorify it again.'"

JOHN 12:27, 28

Fret not today in the midst of sadness.
God meets our needs and restores our gladness.
Sin, sorrow, and suffering sometimes prevail.
Through it all, God cannot fail.
In the midst of trials, we learn compassion.
Be sympathetic; love He does not ration.
We deny self and, to Him, commit.
He always keeps us spiritually fit.
We grow in grace in the midst of our trials.
We are assured that God is good; make no denials.

Today, we may have a sad time.
Joy will come and turn it to a glad time.
In the midst of trouble, He will provide.
Our Lord is forever at our side.
Some events may sometimes be irritating.
Began to live in Christ and don't be hesitating.
There are many suffering in this present world.
Come under God's banner; may His flag be unfurled.
Distressing times in life, we are not despondent.
Christ, within, makes us joy respondent.

Grace for the Present Moment

"We then, as workers together with Him, beseech
you also that ye receive not the grace of God in vain."

II CORINTHIANS 6:1

Our every breath will be a prayer.
His grace is sufficient everywhere.
Unto the Lord, we humbly bow.
The grace He gives is given now.
Moment by moment, the Lord gives us grace.
He helps us to endure each trial we face.
We will draw from His mercy at the time of need.
He helps us now as, to the Spirit, we give heed.
Now is the time to accept His favor.
Taste and see His precious savor.

God's presence is constant.
He makes us competent.
Amazing grace is here and now.
To our loving Savior, we will bow.
Circumstances, don't resent.
Know that the Lord is ever present.
The practice of prayer can be a reflex action.
Drawing from His love brings satisfaction.
God's wisdom has divine power.
God's glory may be revealed this very hour.

Outstanding Individual Liberation

"'Be not afraid of their faces: for I am with thee to deliver thee,' saith the LORD."

JEREMIAH 1:8

Earthly possessions, do not hold dearly.
God sends us where He wants; He guides sincerely.
Wherever we go, God has promised to guard.
He will deliver, though life may be hard.
To our belongings, we don't hold tightly.
When devoted to Him, we will do rightly.
God has promised; He will abide.
In whatever we do, in Him, we'll confide.
Trust in the Lord with all your heart.
From His precepts don't depart.

He is with us to deliver.
Faithfully, He is the Giver.
Our God befriends us;
Then He sends us.
God delivers. He is with you.
Trust in Him to see you through.
Practical understanding is not always right.
Seek God's will first and walk in the light.
Walk down the path that God has appointed.
He assures us that we will not be disappointed.

Understood by God

"Not as though I had already attained, either were already perfect: but I follow after, if that I may apprehend that for which also I am apprehended of Christ Jesus."

PHILIPPIANS 3:12

Give a bold testimony of His divine Power.
God supplies His grace each hour.
Press on to the mark of His high calling.
We are fit for the tasks; He keeps us from falling.
We are called to preach the Good News.
When it is His message, we cannot lose.
We don't have to understand.
We go with God; He holds our hand.
By God, each one is called to preach.
To proclaim His message, He will teach.

Be up and ready.
Have a faith that is steady.
As servants, we wait on the Lord.
Adventurous paths will be explored.
God, the Son, has set us free.
We walk ahead in victory.
Jesus has called us, the Gospel to preach.
The precious Word of God is what we teach.
There is one thing that we must understand:
We are safe and secure in God's holy hand.

Instruction Through Training

"And if thy right hand offend thee, cut it off, and cast it from thee: for it is profitable for thee that one of thy members should perish, and not that thy whole body should be cast into hell."

MATTHEW 5:30

Cast off the sin that hinders your perfection in Christ.
Moral nature is recreated;
His shed blood has sufficed.
God sets limits; He is in control.
It is His desire to make us whole.
When regenerated, lives are altered.
We have abounded in Him, and have not faltered.
How can we improve behavior?
We will trust in Jesus as our Savior.
Every influence of sin must be rejected.
Walk in the Spirit; that is expected.

When sin is detected,
Our path is redirected.
What is lovely in man's sight,
May be ugly in the light.
When we, with the world are flirting,
Trials may come; they are sometimes hurting.
When walking through life
we have sometimes fumbled.
God works best through those
who have been humbled.
When others try to harm us, we do not retaliate.
We let it be known that Jesus is our affiliate.

Respond Quickly

"Agree with thine adversary quickly, whiles thou art
in the way with him; lest at any time the adversary
deliver thee to the judge, and the judge deliver thee to
the officer, and thou be cast into prison."

MATTHEW 5:25

Are you faced with opposition?
Make amends; that's your position.
The laws of God will never change.
Jesus, your life, will rearrange.
Make peace with your brother and come to terms.
The law of love and humility, our Lord confirms.
Wherever there is anger or contention,
Bring it to the Lord's attention.
Pay your debts and heavenly seed sow.
Make peace your goal and God's love bestow.

Live peacefully with each person; hold no grudges.
As you walk in the Spirit, He gently nudges.
Think kind thoughts of those you meet.
Love them, through Christ, and don't retreat.
There are those with a differing opinion.
Let the Word of our Lord have dominion.
Our moral dispositions must not become embittered.
Time is wasted when we have recklessly frittered.
For peace and contentment, we have longed.
Forgive and reconcile to those we have wronged.

July

And ye shall know the truth, and the truth shall make you free. John 8:32

Unavoidable Inspiration

"Verily I say unto thee, 'Thou shalt by no means come out thence, till thou hast paid the uttermost farthing.'"

MATTHEW 5:26

Accept, with faith, each situation.
To covet peace is our vindication.
The Holy Spirit, of sin, will convict.
All evil thoughts and deeds restrict.
Pay attention; to the Holy Spirit, give heed.
To live at peace is what we need.
Give thoughts and plans a thorough review.
Plan to do what God has asked of you.
In prayer and abiding, God's will is sought.
The Spirit prompts; we will do what we ought.

When inspired to do good,
Go and do as you should.
When you think of a kindness to do,
Act upon it; follow through.
Help others to lift their heavy load.
Lord, help us to take the right road.
There is one thing that we must realize:
The Holy Spirit is right here to energize.
We will accomplish; God's plan is not evaded.
Look to the Word; by the Spirit, be persuaded.

Stipulations of a Follower

"If any man come to me, and hate not his father, and
mother, and wife, and children, and brethren, and
sisters, yea and his own life also,
he cannot be My disciple."

LUKE 14:26

To the Holy Spirit, within, be devoted.
May Jesus Christ, the Lord, be promoted.
The love of God is spread abroad in our hearts.
He is consistent; He never departs
A true disciple must be consecrated to Him.
Be a love slave to Jesus, whose light will not dim.
Admiration of Him is expected.
He is exalted and greatly respected.
To the Lord Jesus Christ be always loyal.
Love Him above all others; He is King, most royal.

In Christ, together, be bound.
May our lives in Him be found.
Be not hung up on dogmas,
creeds and organizations.
Our lives should reflect Christ;
we must tell all nations.
God's grace is forever insistent.
To be His disciples, we must be consistent.
Passionate love of the Lord Jesus Christ is imparted.
Our hearts are ablaze with love that is whole-hearted.
The Holy Spirit makes us aware of the minutest sin.
He imparts the compassionate love of God within.

Individual Transgressions

"Then said I, 'Woe is me! For I am undone; because I
am a man of unclean lips, and I dwell in the midst of a
people of unclean lips: for mine eyes have seen the
King, the LORD of hosts.'"

ISAIAH 6:5

The Holy Spirit convicts of sin.
Christ is righteous; He lives within.
One by one each evil deed,
Convicts us of our sin and greed.
God tells us to be holy. Do you hear it?
This is the pleading of the Holy Spirit.
Healing is ours, once convicted.
God's grace avails for those who are afflicted.
Only God can provide the purity demanded.
Purity in our hearts, God has commanded.

When sin gets in the way,
Confess, forsake and pray.
As the doctor: sickness diagnosis,
so the Spirit, sin exposes.
By earthly sin, we all have faulted.
Confess and forsake and the Lord will be exalted.
When we seek His forgiveness,
correction can proceed.
Shortcomings are exposed;
Christ supplies each need.
Repent of all sin and don't be defamed.
God's absolute holiness must be proclaimed.

One of God's No-No's

"Cease from anger, and forsake wrath: fret not thyself
in any wise to do evil."

PSALMS 37:8

Christ's followers have no need to fret.
Just rest in Him and don't forget.
When we are rightly related to God, we rest.
We trust fully in Him, for He knows what is best.
Unbelief is bent toward evil.
Simply trust; may peace be still.
Why become impatient when we can pray?
God's plan unfolds from day to day.
Anxiety in the heart wears a man down.
Turn from worry; wipe away that frown.

God is able; we must remember.
God's love is like a glowing ember.
God's grace is sure to overflow.
We must rest and wait; this we know.
Do not be anxious; this causes harm.
Continue in the Lord; lean on His arm.
Resting depends on a close affinity.
In Christ, we are compatible with divinity.
Depart from evil and do good is a certain requisite.
Trust in the Lord; His rewards are exquisite.

Adapt to God's Purpose

"Commit thy way unto the LORD; trust also in Him;
and He shall bring it to pass."

PSALMS 37:5

Adapt to a purpose, with the kingdom as a goal.
God is preeminent; He saves the soul.
God's resolute must be considered in our estimation.
The kingdom of heaven is our destination.
In everything, put God first.
By evil, be not coerced.
The Lord will give and entirely surpass.
Let not sinful ways trouble and harass.
Is your heart distressed? Don't allow it.
Look for God's peace; He does endow it.

Unto the Lord, plans are committed.
He will bless; His love is transmitted.
With God's purpose and plan in mind,
The greatest joy and peace we find.
God must be at the center of our thoughts and cares.
His own divine love, with all who heed, He shares.
Planning without God's guidance is a mistake.
When we trust in Him, a way, He will make.
Going our own way is like tipping the apple cart.
God has a plan; let Him rule from the heart.

Seeing and Actuality

"And an highway shall be there, and a way,
and it shall be called The way of holiness;
the unclean shall not pass over it; but it shall be for
those: the wayfaring men, though fools,
shall not err therein."

ISAIAH 35:8

Live with eternity's value in view.
Faith in Christ will strengthen you.
It is in the valley, life's lessons are fought.
The vision before us will come when it is sought.
The way of holiness will become clear.
God's plan is fulfilled, when Christ is near.
We will ask the Lord, what we should be.
The pathway is before us; we will follow faithfully.
God has a plan of great appeal.
We walk through the valley; He makes it real.

God gives us a provision,
He sends us on a mission.
To the humble, God gives grace.
He helps us, each trial to face.
Let us seize the opportunity God places before us.
As obedient servants may we
be reliable and laborious.
In the midst of suffering, trying times we will see.
Remember, our Lord gave His life for you and me.
Speak the truth; be bold; the hungry will hear.
We are free to declare His message without fear.

Holy Living Takes Much Giving

"Enter ye in at the strait gate: for wide is the gate,
and broad is the way, that leadeth to destruction, and
many there be which go in thereat: Because strait is
the gate, and narrow is the way, which leadeth unto
life, and few there be that find it."

MATTHEW 7:13, 14a

When we meet a crisis, He will give peace.
Through the grace of God, we will meet it with ease.
How do we cope with each difficult situation?
We overcome by the testimony of our salvation.
The way to destruction is spacious and broad.
Take the narrow way; trust in God.
Our lives are distinguished by our deeds.
Obey the Spirit; that is what one needs.
Enter in at the straight gate.
Come to Jesus; don't procrastinate.

Through difficult times we grow.
We can rejoice; God loves us we know.
This is what the disciple's fast is:
In God's Word, we probe, ponder and practice.
In practical living, we work and do not fear it.
It is a life of overcoming, by the power of the Spirit.
Life, death, blessings and curses are set before us.
Choose God's favor; join heaven's chorus.
Christ completes and perfects; in Him, we abide.
We receive His blessings; in Him, we confide.

The Desire to Be True

"...but as for me and my house, we will serve the LORD."

JOSHUA 24:15

The choice is yours and mine;
let us do His command.
To Him be loyal; His purpose will stand.
O Lord, to serve You, we will choose.
When we will put the Lord first, we will not lose.
We will follow Jesus; that will be our theme.
Only He is King and He reigns supreme.
We choose this day, the Lord to serve.
From His path, we will not swerve.
Of flesh and blood, do not inquire.
We ask of the Lord what is His desire.

The Lord's way we will follow.
In muddy streams, we will not wallow.
Our focus is upon Him, we won't deny.
Follow Him; He will satisfy.
Our choice to serve the Lord is sincere.
His divine will, we will endear.
Determine to go God's way, completely.
Walk with Him each step discretely.
God knows all about us; He knows about the sparrow.
Keep on His course, it is always straight and narrow.

Mighty Thorough Exam

"And if it seem evil unto you to serve the LORD,
choose you this day whom ye will serve; whether
the gods which your fathers served that were on the
other side of the flood, or the gods of the Amorites, in
whose land ye dwell: but as for me and my house,
we will serve the LORD.'

JOSHUA 24:15

God manifests His life in a heart that will trust.
A life that is holy, in Christ, is a must.
Let God's almighty power and might,
Put dreaded thoughts and fears to flight.
He will manifest His life in you.
Yield to Him and let His light shine through.
On God, alone, we will rely.
We attend to the Lord and will not deny.
We will wait upon the Lord because He is God.
Our Heavenly Father will not spare the rod.

His strength avails.
Jesus prevails.
Delight to do His will.
He will provide the skill.
How can we, to the Lord, be more fervent?
Commit your all; then be His servant.
Be totally ready in each situation.
Speak forth His truth about the way of salvation.
We realize that we are safe in His hands.
We lean on Jesus and we know that He understands.

Listless Saints

"And let us consider one another to provoke unto love and good works: Not forsaking the assembling of ourselves together, as the manner of some is; but exhorting one another: and so much the more, as ye see the day approaching."

HEBREWS 10:24, 25

Stir up the coals of love and good works.
A heart filled with Jesus never shirks.
Our Christian friendship, we won't exclude.
We will do our part with joy and gratitude.
Listen for the Lord's heavenly choir.
From helpful deeds we will not retire.
Forsake not Christian friends, but meet together.
Our hearts, in love, He will tether.
The life of Christ is realized,
His holiness is emphasized.

Spur one another toward love and devotion.
He who promised is faithful; He puts us to motion.
From retreat, to advance,
Christian life, we enhance.
With compassionate hearts we are stirred.
We grow spiritually strong through the Word.
Doubt makes things hazy.
We will not be lazy.
We get together to spur one another along.
It may be by encouraging words or by a praise song.

Just Give Me Jesus

"That I may know Him, and the power of His resurrection, and the fellowship of His sufferings, being made conformable unto His death."

PHILIPPIANS 3:10

Fret not about your self esteem.
In Christ, we are on the winning team.
What is most important is to know Him.
He is the Light that won't grow dim.
O Lord, we want to know You better.
Please walk with us and break each fetter.
In whatever we do, may Jesus, our path chart.
He lives within; from Him, we won't part.
Jesus took a towel and began to wash their feet.
In each situation, His mercies we meet.

The world may smirk when they look at us.
On Jesus Christ we should keep our focus.
To know Him is our goal.
He has saved and made us whole.
In every circumstance, may Christ be at the center.
He is our Savior, our Teacher, and our Mentor.
There is an opportunity in every encounter.
Be sure that Christ is the surmounter.
Press on toward the goal; win the supreme prize.
God is calling us upward to our heavenly paradise.

Society's Christian Standard

"Till we all come in the unity of the faith, and of the knowledge of the Son of God, unto a perfect man, unto the measure of the stature of the fullness of Christ."

EPHESIANS 4:13

In Christ, we have been redeemed.
Through a consecrated life, He is esteemed.
For uniqueness and greatness don't compete.
To be in Christ is to be complete.
We are not placed here for remorse or guilt.
The Church of God must be built.
In grace, we grow,
When Christ we know.
How are we fashioned into God's design?
We are a part of His Body; the Lord is divine.

The fullness of Christ is our treasure.
We become mature in Him; it is a pleasure.
What a glorious future.
In Christ, we mature.
Make disciples; help the needy.
With the Gospel, don't be greedy.
Selfish interest, we will put away.
We must build up the Church today.
Our greedy selves, we will abandon.
Christ, the Lord, is our constant companion.

The Value of Spiritual Insight

"In the year that king Uzziah died I saw also the Lord sitting upon a throne, high and lifted up, and his train filled the temple."

ISAIAH 6:1

In every circumstance, choose the Lord; be free.
We live for His kingdom; He gives us victory.
Keep Christ foremost in our vision.
God, alone, shall be our mission.
We, with Christ, are crucified.
Only then, our lives are purified.
God blesses; we will not deny.
It is the Lord that does sanctify.
Give heed in regard to His will and call.
Serve Him in holiness; don't falter and fall.

Listen to His mission; His beckoning calls, receive.
He gives His command; go forth and believe.
To Him, we will implore.
It is Him we adore.
Friends and family may leave us lonely.
It is then we see Jesus only.
Our desire and purpose is Jesus.
He is the only One that will never leave us.
Be willing to obey and do whatever
He has for us to do.
The future belongs to Him; His plan we pursue.

Reckoning With ill-treatment

"But I say unto you, That ye resist not evil: but whosoever shall smite thee on thy right cheek, turn to him the other also."

MATTHEW 5:39

In Christ, we are humble.
Do not, on life's challenges, stumble.
A saint stays sweet, even when insulted.
With the Lord, He has consulted.
We should not insist upon selfish rights.
The Spirit always wins, while the enemy fights.
We will stand and suffer for Jesus' sake.
Our Savior feels each blow we take.
When we are wronged, use no selfish action.
We turn hatred to love; that's our reaction.

When we are Spirit filled,
We do what the Lord has willed.
To the world, we may seem a fool.
Be willing students in God's school.
Be ready to go the second mile.
Face contention with a smile.
Put downs hurt, but we must rise above.
Resist the devil; go God's way; live and love!
When we are under persecution and ridicule,
We need to be sure to follow the Golden Rule.

Straightforward Witness

"I am a debtor both to the Greeks, and to the
Barbarians, both to the wise, and to the unwise."

ROMANS 1:14

To Christ we are forever indebted.
Let His love, in your heart, be embedded.
There is a debt that we all do owe.
We must tell of Christ, that all may know.
To reach the lost should be our goal.
Only God can save our soul.
He saves and keeps; we will express it.
We have been redeemed; we will confess it.
Whatever is of value, we owe to redemption.
We are debtors; there is no exemption.

We are blessed beyond measure.
Christ is our treasure.
The Lord wants us to move ahead.
Worldly pleasures lure; choose Christ instead.
In Christ, there is much satisfaction.
We must put our prayers into action.
Our motivation is our life long debt for our blessing.
Reach out and touch others,
faith in Christ confessing.
Nature bears God's message throughout the earth.
He declares His glory; His gold has much worth.

Supernatural Direction

"If you then, being evil, know how to give good gifts unto your children, how much more shall your Father which is in heaven give good things to them that ask Him?"

MATTHEW 7:11

We trust our Lord; His will we seek.
He is strong and we are weak.
God is the giver of every good thing.
In Him is joy and our hearts sing.
Our Father gives much more than we ask.
He makes us fit for each new task.
In every situation God has control.
We rest in Him; He has made us whole.
Perfect trust will be our attitude.
He leads and guides; we are filled with gratitude.

God gives what is good.
We will do what we should.
To those who ask, good things He gives.
Rise up and praise Him; Jesus lives.
When we received Christ we
become the Father's child.
We trust fully in His grace and will not be defiled.
For daily grace, give Christ all the glory.
All of history is His story.
We make requests in the name of Jesus.
The Father imparts His gifts that please us.

The Wonder of Faith

"And my speech and my preaching were not with
enticing words of man's wisdom, but in demonstration
of the Spirit and of power:"

I CORINTHIANS 2:4

Preach the Good News in the power of the Spirit.
When we are sincere, the hungry will hear it.
Our speech need not be eloquent.
The power of God is excellent
Demonstrate the Holy Spirit's power.
Christ is raised; He's alive this hour
Announce the Gospel of His kingdom.
In Jesus name we will overcome.
To proclaim the Gospel, the Spirit will guide.
In love and obedience, speak the truth;
He will provide.

The entire devil's worldly ways, we deny.
It is the Lord we glorify.
Present the Gospel facts.
We need not perform people pleasing acts.
Believing is the Holy Spirit's work.
From self glory we will shirk.
Clever acts and devices may, to the flesh, appeal.
Gospel truths and sacrifices make
the presentation real.
The Gospel is best preached in a simple manner.
We humbly invite listeners to come under the banner.

Truth of a Firm Persuasion

"And he trembling and astonished said, 'Lord, what wilt thou have me to do?' And the Lord said unto him, 'Arise, and go into the city, and it shall be told thee what thou must do.'"

ACTS 9:6

In Christ our hearts are changed.
Our very nature is rearranged.
Natural man chooses the dark.
Repent; be saved; come into the Ark.
Hate all evil; love what is right.
Receive the Holy Spirit; walk in His light.
With God on the throne, we want to pray.
His grace avails for each new day.
Choose to live by faith; forever hate the wrong.
It is plainly seen that to Jesus we belong.

When we seek to know the Lord,
Our faith is restored.
What is the explanation?
In Christ we are a new creation.
We have a new nature and will go God's way.
Sinful living brings dismay.
Lord, we want to know You more,
Than we have ever known You before.
Jesus is Lord and that is firmly stated.
To God, the Son, we are related.

Supremacy Over Each Follower

"Ye call me Master and Lord; and ye say well;
for so I am."

JOHN 13:13

Our Lord saves from sin's disaster.
He alone is our Holy Master.
We love the Lord; we will obey.
Thou art worthy; we will pray.
Obedience to the Lord is our attitude.
Our hearts are filled with unending gratitude.
To do His will is our desire.
Our Lord is holy; Him, we admire.
He is Lord indeed; He, alone, we nominate.
It is Him that we adore; He does predominate.

We are free to choose.
In Him, we will not lose.
To do His will, we do submit;
Our lives to Him, we commit!
To be a faith-abiding human creature,
We must allow the Lord to be our Teacher.
Our walk with the Lord, we continually examine.
He is always with us through feast or famine.
When committed to the Lord, we need not strive.
We enter into His rest; He is in us and alive.

Supported by His Nearness

"But they that wait upon the LORD shall renew their strength; they shall mount up with wings as eagles; they shall run, and not be weary; and they shall walk, and not faint."

ISAIAH 40:31

On God's presence we depend.
He gives grace and mercy without end.
With the Lord, daily we will talk.
He will show us how to walk.
God is not a counterfeit; He is not fictitious.
Expound the Word and be ambitious.
The Lord is forever our example.
We trust in Him for He is ample.
Hope in the Lord renews our strength.
His mercy stretches to full length.

Always abiding,
In Him, we are confiding.
We will talk along the way,
As we walk with Christ today.
We will be quiet and, for His direction, wait.
Our walk with Him through the Word is great.
Abiding in Jesus is an enriching experience.
Do you feel His Presence? That is obedience!
Our conduct reveals what we have chosen to be.
We cannot live a lie; in Christ we live in victory.

The Entrance to God's Domain

"Blessed are the poor in spirit: for theirs is the
kingdom of heaven."

MATTHEW 5:3

Jesus is our Lord and Master.
Not trusting Him leads to disaster.
Our journey through life is an expedition.
We need Jesus' disposition.
How can we have good behavior?
Accept Jesus today as your Savior.
Jesus came to teach and create.
By His grace, He is adequate.
God's Law is the standard that we try to attain.
In Christ Jesus we rest; in Him we remain.

He is Lord and He provides.
Each moment, He abides.
Jesus is the door.
With open hearts we explore.
Jesus is not just a Teacher who informs.
He is Savior and Lord; He transforms.
In our selfish ways we cannot do it,
Grace avails; each day, He does renew it.
The poor in spirit are not spiritually inferior.
They have learned to know the Lord is superior.

Purification and Freedom from Sin

"For this is the will of God, even your sanctification,
that ye should abstain from fornication."

I THESSALONIANS 4:3

Reckon self dead, be alive in Christ.
His life has thus fully sufficed.
To the Lord, we are consecrated.
Sanctified wholly and emancipated.
Sin and selfishness must die.
It is then that He will sanctify.
With evil, make no compromise.
God knows sin, we can't disguise.
To the Lord alone we will make our plea.
On the throne of the heart, He rules in you and me.

We are free from sin's power,
As we trust His grace this hour.
Be saved, sanctified and healed.
Christ's holy likeness is revealed.
He saves, justifies, and glorifies!
With wondrous beauty, He satisfies.
Selfish interests will have no place.
They will not please God; the cross, we embrace.
Stay away from the evil and self-pleasing ambition.
Meet past errors and wrong doings with contrition.

Imparted Holiness

"But of Him are ye in Christ Jesus, who of God is
made unto us wisdom, and righteousness,
and sanctification, and redemption."

I CORINTHIANS 1:30

In Christ, we will abide.
His grace, He does provide.
The holiness of Christ is yours and mine.
He is real to us; He is divine.
In Christ, God's wisdom is made known.
The way of salvation to us is shown.
Just take what Jesus has imparted.
That is how sanctification is started.
By the power of God, we are delivered and kept.
When the enemy tempts, our Lord will intercept.

It is God's will to set us apart.
New life, in Christ, makes a joyful heart.
His very life, He does expel.
We are set free; in Christ we dwell.
The attributes of Christ are to us imparted.
When we entered by faith, new desires started.
Our hearts are Jesus' habitation.
Sanctification is our expectation.
The heart of a Christian is Jesus' dwelling place.
One day we will see Him face to face.

Temperament and Tasks

"For I say unto you, That except your righteousness
shall exceed the righteousness of the scribes and
Pharisees, ye shall in no case enter into the kingdom
of heaven."

Matthew 5:20

Only in Christ can righteousness reign.
Our selfish works are done in vain.
It is grace that produces good deeds.
His love each Christian needs.
Who, in God's kingdom, will be great?
It is the one whom, for the Lord, does wait.
Christ lives within; each day our grace is new.
Motives are pure; thoughts will be true.
For peace within there is no substitution.
Our moral disposition is our constitution.

What matters is our inner attitude.
In Christ, we live a life of gratitude.
How can our motives be pure?
Ask for forgiveness each day, for sure!
Do not yearn and lament.
Live and enjoy each moment.
To do what is right, we must be what is right.
When abiding in Christ, evil actions take flight.
With God as our Father, what a blessed heredity!
As born again children, we possess divinity.

Does This Give Happiness?

"Blessed are the poor in spirit: theirs is the kingdom of heaven. Blessed are they that mourn: they shall be comforted. Blessed are the meek: they shall inherit the earth. Blessed are they which do hunger and thirst after righteousness: they shall be filled."

MATTHEW 5:3-6

The Beatitudes are dynamic in content.
Its words applied, are par-excellent.
The Lord has given us so much.
The Holy Spirit helps us to keep in touch.
The Lord blesses on each occasion.
He has come to give us consolation.
The Holy Spirit controls our attitudes.
He helps us to receive the beatitudes.
Heed to the Word of His sermon and be blessed.
No greater dogmas have been expressed.

We must trust in Jesus; that is our goal.
The Holy Spirit, within, satisfies our soul.
In the Spirit, our joy is full
The gifts He gives are bountiful.
The blessings God supplies are distinctly expounded.
In His presence, by His gifts we're surrounded.
Sermon on the Mount is His rule; He's our endower.
Awaken us, Lord, to this fact:
The Spirit does empower.
Nations can be ruined by false teaching.
Obey the Lord, our God; we need pure preaching.

The Safeguard of Redemption

"But those things which proceed out of the mouth
come forth from the heart; and they defile the man.
For out of the heart proceed evil thoughts, murders,
adulteries, fornications, thefts, false witness,
blasphemies: These are the things which defile a
man: but to eat with unwashen hands
defileth not a man."

MATTHEW 15:18-20

Look with expectancy towards God's face.
Only Christ can sin erase.
All have sinned and of God's glory fall short.
Christ changes hearts; He's our support.
How can we be undefiled?
Accept Jesus; become God's child.
Things may not be as bad as they seemed.
Through Christ, we've been redeemed.
Redemption, through Christ, is our security.
Life, in the Spirit, is a life of purity.

We share the Good News far and wide.
He is holy; in Him, we abide.
In the dark of night, search for His light.
Our doubts and fears He will put to flight.
As we walk with Him, His joy we share.
His love is present; we are aware.
Our call is to be holy; He is coming for His Bride.
Fear not but just be ready; in Christ, we must abide.
As we walk in the light, we are refreshed.
No longer by sin and the flesh are we enmeshed.

The Route to Understanding

"If any man will do His will, he shall know of the
doctrine, whether it be of God, or whether
I speak of myself."

JOHN 7:17

Be sensitive to the Spirit's voice.
Let obedience be your choice.
Our selfish interests are always wrong.
Adhere to the Word; to the Lord belong.
Yield always to the Golden Rule.
When one rebels, he is a fool.
To believe is to decide to obey.
From His pathway, never stray.
Have you heard the Spirit's call?
Take heed to Him and do not fall.

In constant fellowship, we grow.
Lord, we want to believe and know.
The way to be wise is to comply with His orders.
Always stay within His borders.
Our love for God, with humble service, is proof.
We must not just stand still and be aloof.
When God tells us to go forward, we must go.
We are informed and transformed, His love to show.
Endorse the doctrines that the Word has taught.
When we obey, we will do what we ought.

Submit to His Will; He Will Do

"And straightway He constrained His disciples to get into the ship, and to go to the other side before unto Bethsaida, while He sent away the people."

MARK 6:45

Cherish this moment of time.
Our Lord is the Master, sublime.
The success God leads us to is great.
He has all power; for that there is no debate.
God will fulfill His purpose for us.
Yield to the Spirit; trust in Jesus.
Our success is distinct in God's sight.
He puts us here to be His light.
Jesus' command is to get into the boat.
All will be well; we'll stay afloat.

Prepare,
Then, share.
Don't deplore and lament.
Live in joy for the moment.
May God's purpose become a part of you and me.
When we submit to Him, He supplies the victory.
God's will is not in some far-off future event.
Time spent with Him and for Him is time well-spent.
Sometimes we want to do it later, but God says now.
His will is to be done and He will show us how.

Do You Have Faith?

"Behold, he cometh with clouds; and every eye shall
see Him, and they also which pierced Him: and all
kindreds of the earth shall wail because of Him.
Even so, Amen."

REVELATION 1: 7

In the midst of distress, God will act.
He will teach us; that is a fact.
Through troubles and trials, our faith increases.
God's presence is real; His love never ceases.
Has sorrow, grief and suffering crossed your path?
God meets us in the darkest wrath.
Through difficult times, God is right there.
Be still and know that He hears your prayer.
Clouds are for a purpose; do not fear.
Just put your trust in Him; He is ever near.

In child-like trust,
Believe, though winds may gust.
Though difficult times appear,
We know God is near.
Beyond the clouds, the sun is shining.
In the midst of our sorrow, the Lord is refining.
Cloudy skies tell of sorrow and fright.
Through the clouds, Jesus makes all things right.
The Lord knows what is in the heart of man.
He sees not as man sees; redemption is His plan.

A Definite Decree About His Methods

"But Jesus did not commit Himself unto them,
because He knew all men, and needed not that any
should testify of man: for He knew what was in man."

JOHN 2: 24, 25

Lord, help us to listen and obey.
As you lead, step by step each day.
The Lord will give to us a mission field.
We must go and tell; to His voice, we will yield.
With criticism, do not flirt.
Discern what is needed and keep your spirit alert.
The Lord will return; tell others to believe.
Teaching and instruction, we will receive.
After prayer and contemplation,
He will deliver us from temptation.

Wait on the Lord; the Word has been spoken.
The Spirit will move on hearts that are broken.
God's love is evident.
In Him, we are confident.
We have come to this conclusion:
To trust in man, leads to confusion.
We put our trust in God, not in carnal man.
In faith, we fit into God's plan.
In the presence of God, we will be content.
Our associations with others are a sacred intent.

Totally Sanctified

"But let him ask in faith, nothing wavering. For he
that wavereth is like a wave of the sea driven with the
wind and tossed."

JAMES 1:6

Toe the line; we must be accurate.
God's Word is truth; He is articulate.
Our entire nature is cleansed and refreshed.
We are free in the Spirit and not enmeshed.
The Lord continues to inspire,
The changes He wants will be entire.
In whatever you do, do it with your might.
Persevere to the end as you do what is right.
Be complete in Him and not defective.
We will learn His ways and be effective.

To have an effect,
Let Jesus perfect.
Fully surrender your heart, holding nothing back.
Our faults will diminish with no lack.
God knows everything about us.
Our only perfection is in Jesus.
He works within us to finish and complete.
Wholeheartily, be willing, to wash your brother's feet.
The Holy Spirit detects our defects.
Sin and sadness, He rejects

August

Then saith He unto His disciples, The harvest truly is plenteous, but the labourers are few; Pray ye therefore the Lord of the harvest, that He will send forth labourers into His harvest.
Matthew 9:37

The One Who Satisfies, Sanctifies

"And it came to pass, when Jesus had made an end
of commanding His twelve disciples, He departed
thence to teach and to preach in their cities."

MATTHEW 11:1

Who are we, to be a cynic?
Jesus is the Healer at every clinic.
Jesus is my Lord and Master.
Only He can save us from disaster.
Jesus is the only One who can satisfy.
God is able; we will testify.
To put your trust in man is weak.
Trust the Lord; for no one else seek.
The heart of man is deceptive.
Of God's grace and mercy, we're receptive.

Jesus understands what we go through.
We are confident in what He can do.
You will not be bored,
If you wait on the Lord.
We must learn to do what we are told.
When we obey, God makes us bold.
Boldly, we come before the throne.
Wait there until His will is shown.
There are times to be silent and to the Spirit awake.
Learn much from His Word; go forth for Jesus' sake.

Taught By Tribulation

"These things I have spoken unto you, that in Me ye might have peace. In the world ye shall have tribulation: but be of good cheer; I have overcome the world."

JOHN 16:33

In the midst of trials, Jesus is right there.
He bestows on us His loving care.
Our faith in God will be expressed.
We will meet with trouble, but not be depressed.
Though plagues surround, we will not fear.
We have God's strength, He is ever near.
Trials come, but we face each one.
Be of good cheer; we have strength in His Son.
Take heart; trust the Lord to overcome;
The world around us is troublesome.

Be not anxious; in Him we rest.
Trials will come; we will do our best.
He sees us through trials.
We make no denials.
In the midst of troubles, be not disturbed.
The Lord has an answer; In Him, sin is curbed.
When difficulties make us feel crushed,
Our hope is in God and in Him we trust.
When faced with conflict and adverse situations.
Keep the peace; yield not to consternations.

The Superpower of Jehovah

"Then He took unto Him the twelve, and said unto them, 'Behold, we go up to Jerusalem, and all things that are written by the prophets concerning the Son of man shall be accomplished.'"

LUKE 18:31

Jesus came to do the Father's will.
He died on the cross, our redemption to fulfill.
Steadfastly aim for the goal.
The Lord has saved; He has made whole.
We commit our all to Him and see,
The blessings He prepared for you and me.
He took our sins and carried our sorrows.
He intercedes throughout our tomorrows.
What He has written, shall come to pass.
Rebuke all evil that tries to harass.

Once saved, worldly passions we are now repelled.
God has a purpose; we are compelled.
Help us clear our lives of clutter.
No longer will it be a mess to mutter.
With the Lord, we are co-workers.
God has a plan for our lives; we won't be shirkers.
We must clear our thoughts of what is bleak.
Let us wholesome statements speak.
As a servant, the Lord Jesus Christ is exalted.
We follow His example and selfish acts are halted.

The Close Relationship of Jehovah

"Then He took unto Him the twelve, and said unto them, 'Behold, we go up to Jerusalem, and all things that are written by the prophets concerning the Son of man shall be accomplished.'"

LUKE 18:31

We have nothing to offer, only to yield.
Christ is within; by His Spirit we are sealed.
Of our attributes, we do not boast.
We belong to Jesus; He does the most.
In Him, we will proudly rejoice.
He is our wisdom; He is our only choice.
There is nothing that we can bring.
He paid it all; to Him we cling.
Prophetic scriptures, daily, are coming true.
His promises are many, not few.

In Christ we abide.
There's no room for foolish pride.
May egocentric deeds be past.
What is done through Christ will last.
When selfish whims are extinguished,
God's almighty power is distinguished.
God molds a royal vessel out of clay.
We must be pliable to Him each day.
Self-sufficiency must flee; He abides in you and me.
Our relationship with Christ will lead us on to victory.

The Confusing Summoning of Jehovah

"And they shall scourge Him, and put Him to death:
and the third day He shall rise again. And they
understood none of these things: and this saying was
hid from them, neither knew they the things which
were spoken."

LUKE 18:33, 34

God's intentions are always good; He will suggest.
When we heed His call, we will be blessed.
Simply rest in the Father's care.
He is with us everywhere.
We do not need to comprehend.
Trust Him; merely take His hand.
We know not what the Lord has in store.
All we need to do is trust Him more.
Each one has marching orders.
God leads His flock within His borders.

In His will,
He will fulfill.
In His Presence,
Is sweet essence.
God's will is in the now.
We need not wonder how.
He has everything in control.
Christ paid the price to save the soul.
The Holy Scriptures we will ponder.
The Word of God makes love grow fonder.

A Symbol of Suffering in Intercession

"At that day ye shall ask in my name: and I say not
unto you, that I will pray the Father for you:"

JOHN 16:26

To be one with Christ is our desire.
His own attributes we acquire.
Nothing of self or sin do we render.
Only to Christ and the cross, we surrender.
Worldly ways, we do defy.
With Christ, we identify.
We will ask of the Father in Jesus name.
To live for His glory is why we came.
To gain peace in Him, is not a loss.
Christ's sacrifice removed our dross.

God gives grace
In each trial we face.
Pray to keep healthy.
It will keep us spiritually wealthy.
Our prayers are petitions in Jesus' name.
Keep His Word alive, it is a living flame.
Pray, rejoice and give thanks.
Nothing else outshines or outranks.
Our prayers may be answered differently.
God's answer is right and we respect Him reverently.

Ask; the Father Rules the Household

"And He said unto them, 'How is it that ye sought Me?
Wist ye not that I must be about
My Father's business?'"

LUKE 2:49

In the Father's house we do abide.
Amazing grace, He does provide.
This world's wealth we won't possess;
We must be about the Father's business.
In the Son of God there is perfect union.
Moment by moment, there is sweet communion.
Our Father's house is where we want to be.
We live and move in His abiding reality.
Oh, Lord, we want You to have Your way.
Be present in our lives today.

God hears when our heart cries out.
The quiet whisper has the loudest shout.
We know, by God, our voice is heard.
We pray according to His Word.
In the Father's house, what is done is right.
We love and serve the Lord with all our might.
A well prepared meal is a joy in which to partake.
As we dwell in God's presence,
His blessings we take.
We read the Word and take lessons from the Savior.
He is the One who imparts holy behavior.

Ask, That He Be Glorified

"And the angel answered and said unto her, 'The Holy
Ghost shall come upon thee, and the power of the
Highest shall overshadow thee; therefore also that
Holy thing which shall be born of thee shall be called
the Son of God.'"

LUKE 1:35

God is our Father; to Him, we are related.
Our hearts are clean; our souls are elated.
The Son of God is born within.
He is formed in us and frees from sin.
We must be doing our Father's will.
The cup of blessing, He will fill.
May the Son of God be manifest.
He enables us to pass each test.
Be not involved in the world's busyness.
Be about the Father's business.

We are children of the King.
We will trust in Him for everything.
Be child like in your attitude.
A child of God is full of gratitude.
For God's purposeful plan, be enthused.
Walk in the Word and be not confused.
Live Christ's life; He lives in you.
When born again, He makes all things new.
God's peace and justice will never be destroyed.
With no end to His reign, His zeal, we can't avoid.

Intercede; God Hears Our Need

"Then they took away the stone from the place where the dead was laid. And Jesus lifted up His eyes, and said, 'Father, I thank Thee that Thou hast heard Me.'"

JOHN 11:41

In the name of Jesus, we will pray.
God, the Father, will hear what we say.
The Holy Spirit, in the Christian, dwells.
We pray to the Father; our Lord excels.
A prayer in the Spirit, the Father endears.
He removes our doubts and fears.
We are changed by the Spirit.
We pray, and the Father will hear it.
The Father answers the prayer of His Son.
How thankful we are that we are one.

In His presence we rest.
He does what is best.
We are miraculously vessels of clay.
Mold us and make us after Your way.
We thank the Lord; He has heard us.
We can go on our way and be victorious.
Be one with Christ to be effective.
Supernatural sense is not defective.
The Lord is the Life and Light to every nation.
He imparts to us new birth and gives to us salvation

Belonging to the Pious

"Wherefore let them that suffer according to the will of God commit the keeping of their souls to Him in well doing, as unto a faithful Creator."

I PETER 4:19

Our souls, to God, we will commit.
To His will, we will submit.
Our strength and courage are not deprived.
Through suffering, we have survived.
God wants us to bloom where we are planted.
His grace and mercy, He has granted.
Commit yourself to your Creator.
There is no one who could be greater.
Continue, always, to do well.
He helps us more that we can tell.

The Spirit gives wisdom and understanding.
We will do what He is commanding.
We are not self sufficient.
Jesus, our Lord, is efficient.
We are united with Him in resurrection power.
We grow and are strengthened hour by hour.
When we make a difference in other people's lives,
We rejoice in our sufferings and our spirit revives.
Whatever the Lord permits to happen, we will accept.
If we do wrong, the Holy Spirit will intercept.

The Personal Proof is Essential

"And Elisha saw it, and he cried, "'My father, my
father, the chariot of Israel, and the horsemen
thereof.'" And he saw him no more: and he took hold
of his own clothes, and rent them in two pieces."

II KINGS 2:12

We cannot depend on Elijah's merit.
We must go forth; have faith and share it.
The Lord has promised that we will not walk alone.
I'll trust Him; He's the cornerstone.
Be strong in the Lord and in the power of His might.
Keep your eyes upon Him and do not lose sight.
We will be caught up to meet Him.
Christ will return and we will greet Him.
The experience must come; we move ahead.
Trust not in yourself, but in Jesus instead.

This is what the fact is:
We will put God's plan into practice.
When your mentor does depart,
Just trust the Lord with all your heart.
Christian friends enrich our lives.
It is the Spirit that revives.
What a blessing a godly teacher is to one who learns.
What has been taught yields great returns.
From the mountaintop to the valley He takes us.
He is the One who never leaves us or forsakes us.

God, Man and His Peace

"And He saith unto them, 'Why are ye fearful, O ye of little faith?' Then He arose, and rebuked the winds and the sea; and there was a great calm."

MATTHEW 8:26

In Christ, we have confidence.
Rely on his providence.
The Lord always meets us in the crisis hour.
He endues us with His power.
He gives us faith; we won't deny.
Fully trust and on Him rely.
We rest in Him; He has control.
Fear not; He has made us whole.
To be without blame is to be God's best.
Only in Jesus, will we find true rest.

In the midst of turbulence, in Him be confident.
The Lord gives us what is best; this is evident.
We will not be afraid.
In the Lord, our trust is laid.
The truth of the Word, we will distinguish.
The Holy Spirit's fire, we will not extinguish.
Real rest comes when we are in the midst of conflict.
It is then that the enemy we must contradict.
Would we be lacking faith, when timid and afraid?
Resist the enemy in Jesus' name;
He comes to your aid.

Don't Put Out the Spirit's Fire

"Quench not the Spirit."

1 THESSALONIANS 5:19

Listen intently to the voice of the Spirit.
He speaks softly, but you will hear it.
The voice of the Spirit is like a gentle breeze.
Yield to His advice; your burdens He will ease.
It is very important to right the wrong.
It is then we can meet the next crisis with a song.
Through troubled times, He will guide.
He whispers peace; in Him, abide.
Quench not the Spirit; He will direct.
His compelling voice, we must detect.

The Lord speaks that we may know.
All hindering spirits, in the name of Jesus, must go.
For God's perfect will be yearning.
Be vigilant and discerning.
Walk in the Spirit; make that your pursuit.
It is in Him that we bear fruit.
God gives to us what He knows is best.
Though storms may come, in Him, we rest.
When we retreat, the Spirit will persist.
God gives His orders; all saints enlist.

Correcting By Punishment

"And ye have forgotten the exhortation which speaketh unto you as unto children, 'My son, despise not thou the chastening of the Lord, nor faint when thou art rebuked of Him.'"

HEBREWS 12:5

Don't meet rebuke with disappointment.
Heed to God's divine appointment.
The wisdom of God, we will not deny.
Through chastening, He will sanctify.
To be set apart is our utmost goal.
As we yield, He keeps us whole.
Don't lose heart when you are corrected.
Exalt Christ, the resurrected!
Oh Lord, grip us by Your power.
Do Your work through us this hour.

We will be His delight,
When we walk in His light.
God's will, may be hastened,
When we have been chastened.
The subduing He does, we will accept.
It draws us closer to Him; our faith is kept.
Only Christ can change darkness into light.
We will love the Lord with all of our might.
He endured the cross; give heed to His direction.
He is our Savior and Lord; He imparts perfection.

Quality Mark of Salvation

"Marvel not that I said unto thee,
'Ye must be born again.'"

JOHN 3:7

To be born again means new life in Jesus.
His righteousness, alone, will please us.
We are born anew and have spiritual vision.
The Spirit reigns, the kingdom is our mission.
We have received His nature and can see His rule.
We behold His stature as Master of our school.
On the Holy Spirit we depend.
Jesus is our Savior and our friend.
Say no to sinful lust and pleasure.
Turn to the Lord; He is our treasure.

When we obey Him, we need not sin.
We have the life of Christ within.
The slightest sin may be detected.
May His glory, always be reflected.
When we try to control our lives, it is a disaster.
We must put our trust in Him, our Lord and Master.
When Jesus is in full control,
We walk in His path and He keeps us whole.
As a new creation, we have a new beginning.
The Holy Spirit, within, gives power to stop sinning.

Is He Aware of My Presence?

"To Him the porter openeth; and the sheep hear His voice: and He calleth His own sheep by name, and leadeth them out."

JOHN 10:3

Dogma and creed, alone, will fail.
The love of the Master does prevail.
Jesus, Himself, gives us instruction.
The Master keeps us in production.
Some things are hard to understand.
We simply need to take His hand.
He calls His own sheep by name.
To follow the Shepherd is our aim.
Indescribably precious is His touch.
The Lord loves us very much.

The Lord, divine,
Says, You are mine.
He calls us by name,
To save us, He came.
The Lord knows all about us and He has plans.
Our needs He meets in each circumstance.
The Lord formed us for a purpose that is particular.
We have His favor; the future is spectacular.
Do we know the Savior or just know doctrine?
Grace and mercy, through Christ, is genuine.

Deterred In Consecration

"Now when Jesus heard these things, He said unto
him, 'Yet lackest thou one thing: sell all that thou
hast, and distribute unto the poor, and thou shalt have
treasure in heaven: and come, follow Me.'"

Luke 18:22

Sometimes, the Lord gives strict demands.
We must yield to His commands.
Listen and follow with devotion.
Put His request into motion.
God tells us we should not be discouraged.
He gives His Word; we are encouraged.
He tells us to come and follow Him;
His words are stern.
We will obey; for Him, we yearn.
The Word of God will not return void.
When the Spirit calls, do not avoid.

Jesus wants us to surrender all.
Expect this response when, on Him, you call.
God's Word stands.
His kingdom expands.
To be healthy,
Be spiritually wealthy.
Eternal life avails for all who desire salvation.
A full surrender is a sincere confirmation.
Faith in Christ is our most precious possession.
Repent and believe; salvation is our confession.

Many Blessings! Much Is Demanded

"And when he heard this,
he was very sorrowful; for he was very rich."

LUKE 18:23

The Word of the Lord will set us free.
He brings release, when we agree.
Though sorrow may come, do not waiver.
Unending yearning and faith will bring us favor.
To the Lord, Himself, we will be devoted.
Selfishness must be demoted.
The Word of the Lord may sometimes be stern.
We will obey; for His will we yearn.
Hold not tight to what you have possessed.
To have earthly treasure, be not obsessed.

Listen to His voice
Make His will your choice.
Our God will enable.
He makes our paths stable.
Our walk with the Lord must be real and not phony.
Selfishness and pride will hinder our testimony.
With joy, we will respond to the Lord's command.
We will partner with Him and He will hold our hand.
Our sins He took away; He intercedes each day.
We are in right standing; we believe and pray.

Awareness of One's Personal Interest

"Come unto Me, all ye that labour and are heavy
laden, and I will give you rest."

MATTHEW 11:28

Reckon that your old nature is dead.
Take on the life of Christ instead.
In the Lord Jesus Christ we are complete.
He abides within, with each trial we meet.
The enemy tries to burden and enmesh.
Always come to Jesus and He will refresh.
Selfish desires have been put away.
We rest in Jesus and go His way.
All our wrongs must be made right.
Coming to Jesus puts sin to flight.

God's Word stands.
Obey His commands
In our quiet times,
The Lord, our life, refines.
Jesus says, "Come to Me."
In Him, there is victory.
There is only one profound solution.
Life, in Christ, is our reliable absolution.
Die to self and to the Lord be true.
Love will prevail and greedy acts subdue.

Fulfillment

"Blessed are the poor in spirit: for theirs is the
kingdom of heaven."

MATTHEW 5:3

Jesus makes our lives complete.
With the world, we need not compete.
Because Christ is all in all, there's no need to fear.
We know that every prayer He will hear.
God answers prayers in His own way.
His grace and mercy He does relay.
Let Jesus be your all in all.
He'll lift you up; you will not fall.
In His perfect time, God will answer prayer.
We know He's present everywhere.

Rest in Him and be secure.
Jesus, help us to endure.
God gives us what is best.
He gives us peaceful rest.
In Christ, we are made whole.
He gives new life and saves our soul.
Evil lurks around, but do not fret.
Be certain that the Lord will meet each threat.
We are richly blessed when self is insignificant.
We have God's blessing and favor; He is magnificent.

Serving Without a Review

"I indeed baptize you with water unto repentance:
but He that cometh after me is mightier than I, whose
shoes I am not worthy to bear: He shall baptize you
with the Holy Ghost, and with fire:"

MATTHEW 3:11

Unto Christ, our Savior, yield.
We are co-laborers in His field.
A born again life in Christ, peace brings.
Never lacking, our heart sings.
Blessed are the poor in spirit.
They listen for God's voice and hear it.
Let your goodness be inspired.
His kingdom is to be admired.
Oh how we need the Holy Spirit's power.
We admit our need and trust Him hour by hour.

To Him we yield;
We are, with the Spirit, sealed.
Believers in Christ are not inferior.
The Holy Triune God is superior.
Jesus calls us; we submit.
Our lives to Him, we do commit.
In common things, the Lord has inspired.
A fellow-worker with God has grace acquired.
We are endued with sacred
influence beyond measure.
In Him, we are sanctified;
it is His life that we treasure.

Not I, But It Is the Lord

"I indeed baptize you with water unto repentance:
but He that cometh after me is mightier than I, whose
shoes I am not worthy to bear: He shall baptize you
with the Holy Ghost, and with fire:"

MATTHEW 3:11

The Holy Spirit convicts of sin.
How we need His life, within.
When filled with anxiety and despair,
The Lord sheds His light and shows His care.
Not I, but Christ, be exalted.
Only in the flesh I've faulted.
When it is the Lord, alone, that we desire,
He will baptize us with fire.
The baptism in the Spirit is for all ages.
It is written in the Holy Pages.

Unworthy are we.
In Christ, we are free.
With the Holy Spirit, He does baptize.
It is then His power we realize.
It is no longer ourselves, but He.
It is then that we live in victory.
In the true Church of God, let there be no division.
Christ, Himself, is the Head; His love is the provision.
Empty, meaningless, selfish phrases are to no avail.
Prayers from the heart with sincere desire will not fail.

Selection and Struggle

"But when ye pray, use not vain repetitions, as the heathen do; for they think that they shall be heard for their much speaking."

MATTHEW 6:7

The secret closet is a place of prayer.
We can always meet our Father there.
When alone with God in the secret place,
He enables us each task to face.
In our prayer, we are secure.
God is able; we are sure.
Find a place to be with God alone.
He cares very much for His own.
God gives a listening ear to all that we say.
His love and compassion will brighten each day.

Shut the door.
Then, implore.
Pray in the secret place
His divine presence, embrace.
Close the closet door and be not distracted.
Draw near to God; to Him be attracted.
Our fellowship with Christ should be steadfast.
There are many distractions; never put Him last.
Release your thoughts from all that will divert.
Jesus only is sought and He does convert.

Unworldly Manifestation

"Or what man is there of you, whom if his son ask
bread, will he give him a stone?"

MATTHEW 7:9

Righteousness, through Christ, has much avail.
Constantly abide in Him; He will not fail.
If it is His will, God gives what we ask.
He makes us fit for every task.
Be fervent in spirit and in prayer.
Put God first, and His gospel share.
When a brother or sister asks us for bread,
We do not give them a stone instead.
We receive God's blessings as we walk in His light.
Obedience is precious in God's sight.

I am God's child.
I am no longer defiled.
Remember to seek Him, and then ask.
Obedience is our task.
Disobedience is like betrayal with a kiss.
When we pray, we must not ask amiss.
A child will reflect the parent's nature.
May we become, through Christ, mature.
God's directing sign is a standard that is fixed.
It is morally good and not with evil mixed.

Bearing Fruit While Being Friends

"Henceforth I call you not servants; for the servant knoweth not what his lord doeth: but I have called you friends; for all things that I have heard of My Father I have made known unto you."

JOHN 15:15

Complete surrender with nothing held back,
Helps us bear fruit with no lack.
Jesus is our Friend; together we bear fruit.
His amazing grace is absolute!
By the Lord, we have been appointed.
Simply trust in the anointed.
Jesus said I have called you friends.
The love He gives never ends.
Oh, my God, I delight to do Your will.
Your purpose for me, You will fulfill.

Our Friend, Jesus, is a priceless treasure.
He loves us beyond measure.
To do God's will is our delight.
What He wants is always right.
In this life, we will encounter battles and conflict.
God see us through it; this is His edict.
Have no affinity with the sinful past.
Do the will of God; the privilege is vast.
Our agreement with Christ has a common purpose.
He is a valuable Friend,
the One who gives us impetus.

Are You Agitated?

"Peace I leave with you, my peace I give unto you:
not as the world giveth, give I unto you. Let not your
heart be troubled, neither let it be afraid."

JOHN 14:27

Inner peace must come from Jesus.
He is the only One that will please us.
Our Lord's words are spirit and life.
He gives peace instead of strife.
The peace of God has set us free.
We walk by faith and liberty.
Confirming peace from Jesus receive.
The Words He speaks, we do believe.
Think not on what does disturb.
Think of Jesus; He is superb.

In Christ, we have peace.
He brings sweet release.
In Him we rest.
He gives what is best.
In a troubled spirit, there is no peace.
Put your trust in the Lord; He brings release.
Jesus gives righteousness, peace and joy.
He will not let the enemy destroy.
We have eternity ahead to consider.
Jesus atoning blood is the only sin-ridder.

Relations with God and Man, Active

Then Jesus said unto them, "Yet a little while is the light with you. Walk while ye have the light, lest darkness come upon you: for he that walketh in darkness knoweth not whither he goeth."

JOHN 12:35

What we need, the Lord supplies.
All born again believers, on Christ relies.
Faith in God, we must confess.
Even when we are in the valley, His life profess.
In Him, believe and on Him, rely.
Faith is infinite; it will not die.
To express love is God's desire.
His grace and mercy we aspire.
The Lord wills that we be blessed.
First, our faith is put to the test.

Let your faith be confessed.
Let not doubts be expressed.
Circumstances may discourage.
Faith avails to give us courage.
We want to know His Word, His will and His mind.
The sinful past we will leave behind.
The atonement is life's scorecard.
Rest in His grace; this is not hard.
Self gratification will not produce moral excellence.
Indifference to God's Word leads to moral negligence.

Profit by Petitioning

"And it came to pass, that, as He was praying in a certain place, when He ceased, one of His disciples said unto Him, 'Lord, teach us to pray, as John also taught his disciples.'"

LUKE 11:1

Prayer can change our attitude,
From complaints into gratitude.
The life of Christ is fed by prayer.
He will, with us, each burden share
Through prayer our lives are nourished.
Those who feasted on His Word have flourished.
It is important to learn how to pray.
God will instruct us from day to day.
Prayer will change our way of thinking.
From His fountain, keep on drinking.

With the Father, constantly converse.
Praise God's name in song and verse.
We are abundantly blessed.
In faith, prayers are confessed.
Prayer works wonders in a man's disposition.
From sadness to joy, one goes on a mission.
For prayer to be effective,
Our lives must not be defective.
Our lives He will enhance.
We must give Jesus Christ a chance.

Awe-inspiring Closeness

"Jesus saith unto her, 'Said I not unto thee that,
if thou wouldest believe, thou shouldest
see the glory of God?'"

JOHN 11:40

What I need, the Lord supplies.
Every saint, on Christ, relies.
Faith in God, we must confess.
Even in the valley, His life we profess.
In Him believe and on Him rely.
Faith is right and will never die.
To express love is God's desire.
His grace and mercy we aspire.
The Lord wills that we be blessed.
First, our faith is put to a test.

Let your faith be fervent.
From past vices repent.
Some things may be hard to bear.
Our Lord will help; He is right there.
By the fountain of joy, we are continually refreshed.
No longer are we, by the world's ways enmeshed.
Today is a special gift and we have been given much.
We are blessed by the Master's touch.
Conflicting ideas are part of the enemy's plot.
Our loyalty is tested; God's truth must be sought.

Am I Brought to Belief by the Lord?

"Behold, I give unto you power to tread on serpents
and scorpions, and over all the power of the enemy:
and nothing shall by any means hurt you.
Notwithstanding in this rejoice not, that the spirits are
subject unto you; but rather rejoice, because your
names are written in heaven."

LUKE 10:19, 20

In heaven, my name is written down.
Having Christ within, I no longer frown.
My home is in heaven; I'll rejoice.
Jesus reigns supreme; He is my choice.
From glory to glory He changes me.
Life is abundant; He has set free.
Rejoice that your name is written in heaven above.
This is made true, because of Christ's love.
Put your trust in the Lord; that is firmly stated.
To our Lord Jesus Christ be rightly related.

In Him, we rest.
He does what is best.
Press on toward the goal.
In Christ, we are whole.
I desire that in His house I may reside.
How pleasant it is when, in Him, I abide.
There is delight to be to Christ related.
Pure joy presides and I feel elated.
We are enrolled in heaven; in Him there is authority.
Fear not; live in victory; one with Him is a majority.

His Jubilation, My Jubilation

"These things have I spoken unto you, that My joy
might remain in you, and that your joy might be full."

JOHN 15:11

Lord, I delight to do Your will.
As I trust, my cup You will fill.
How blessed I am to have His joy.
The cares of the world will not annoy.
In Christ, I will live and He does inspire.
His holy life, He does bequeath and require.
I will not strive for honor or fame.
The joy of the Lord, I will proclaim.
A Christian manifests a life supernatural.
To walk in love is, to the Christian, natural.

We will proclaim Jesus name when
facing a mountain.
Living Water flows from the fountain.
By this spring of joy, we are continually refreshed.
No longer are we, by the world's ways enmeshed.
God does great things that
are sometimes undetected.
His will is accomplished, but not how we expected.
Our joy and gladness is complete and overflowing.
The Word of God is fulfilled; our faith keeps growing.
The glory of God is our sincere desire.
In one accord with Him, we can sing in His choir.

September

Which also said, Ye men of Galilee, why stand ye gazing up into heaven? this same Jesus, which is taken up from you into heaven, shall so come in like manner as ye have seen Him go into heaven. Acts 1:11

Unstained and Pure

"Because it is written, 'Be ye holy; for I am holy.'"

I PETER 1:16

In Christ, we are related to the Father.
He gives His attributes and no other.
The purpose of life is to be holy.
This means He is present, wholly.
To God's holiness, be attracted.
Vow to never be distracted.
Christians can remain holy and pure,
When Christ lives within, because His ways are sure.
To God, our Father, we are related.
We were made to be holy; for this we were created.

Holiness is our fore-ordained lot.
May God's perfect will be sought.
He makes us to be whole.
Love with heart, mind and soul.
God is holy; live for His glory.
Be pure, in Christ; that is the Gospel story.
Purity in the life of a Christian is manifested.
Because of the atonement,
we need not be sin infested.
When, to Jesus Christ, we are to others introducing
We know that good fruit He will be producing.

The Solemn Oath of Consecration

"He that believeth on Me, as the scripture hath said,
out of his belly shall flow rivers of living water."

JOHN 7:38

God pours out His love and from us it flows.
Our love for others grows and grows.
Our worth is not measured by success.
We are complete in Christ; this, we confess.
Become mature in Jesus' stature.
In Him, be confident and secure.
The streams of water are an unfailing source.
God's will and blessing is the guiding course.
Once we have of living water tasted,
The love poured out is never wasted.

May His Word flow,
That all may know.
Make, in us, a vessel poured,
That we may magnify the Lord.
When trials come, may complaints be hushed.
The fragrance is sweet when the flower is crushed.
What God supplies, we cannot assess.
He sends us out to share what we possess.
Come to the fountain; blessing He will bestow.
Springs of living water shall continually flow.

Irrigating to Free From Doubt

"And the three mighty men brake through the host of
the Philistines, and drew water out of the well of
Bethlehem, that was by the gate, and took it, and
brought it to David: nevertheless he would not drink
thereof, but poured it out unto the LORD."

II SAMUEL 23:16

Love, friendship and spiritual
blessings are given away.
They are from God; we will confess this each day.
Blessings are from God and He cares.
He gives freely because He cares.
What we have, we will give.
Share the Gospel, that others may live.
God pours out His blessings and gifts.
As we share, many burdens He lifts.
Have you received a blessing to share?
He wants His goodness shed everywhere.

Blessings distributed,
To God is attributed.
Living water must flow.
We participate, that others may know.
May this word from your lips be confessed:
We will pour out our lives, for God has blessed.
We must be generous without excuse.
What we keep for ourselves, we will lose.
A well watered garden will produce healthy fruit.
Offering praise to God is a worthwhile pursuit.

To Him We Belong

"I have manifested Thy name unto the men which
Thou gavest Me out of the world: Thine they were,
and Thou gavest them Me; and they have
kept Thy Word."

JOHN 17:6

To Him we belong.
He makes us strong.
We are not our own; we are His.
One, with the Lord, is heavenly bliss.
When we meet temptation or disaster,
We must remember Jesus is our Master.
To belong to Him is to be spiritually noble.
Go with His message; make it global.
We are cleansed by His blood and forgiven.
His disciples, unto Him, are given.

What heavenly joy it is to know,
We are accepted in the Beloved here below.
We do not belong to selfish wishes.
We are craving heavenly dishes.
This is a secure fact: We are His own.
We praise You, Lord; may Your presence be shown.
The love God gives will never cease.
Help us, Lord, faith to increase.
The Word of God is a treasure; it is read and heard.
Believers give rich advice; this belt of truth will gird.

Dedicated Watchfulness

"And He cometh unto the disciples, and findeth them asleep, and saith unto Peter, 'What, could ye not watch with Me one hour?'"

MATTHEW 26:40

For the Lord, we will watch and wait.
His quick return, we will celebrate.
It is hard for us to understand,
As we keep guard, we hold His hand.
Will Jesus come and find us sleeping?
Will He praise our careful keeping?
The spirit is willing, but the flesh is weak.
Be fully surrendered; the Lord's will seek.
Can we watch for Him this hour?
Look up and wait; He will come with power.

Rise and let us with the Gospel go.
Then the world of darkness will know.
With worldly ways, do not flirt.
Be ready and expectant and be alert.
With Jesus, a vigil we will keep.
Be always vigilant and do not fall asleep.
God is at work in hearts that are ready.
We joyfully minister; our purpose is steady.
Jesus died, arose, ascended and sent the Holy Spirit.
What a blessing we have; what a profitable benefit.

The Father's Enduring Love

Expanding God's Kingdom

"He that believeth on Me, as the scripture hath said,
'Out of his belly shall flow rivers of living water.'"

JOHN 7:38

Glory to God! We are confessing.
What we do and say shall be a blessing.
Give what you have and it will increase.
A river of blessing will not cease.
We do not know how many lives we touch.
Living water will accomplish much.
The fountain from believers will flow.
There is healing in the Gospel, that all may know.
Troubles try to block His path.
We'll understand in the aftermath.

Like a river,
Be a giver!
Through heavenly channels, living waters flow.
Be a blessing to all and watch faith grow.
Jesus is the One who satisfies our thirst.
He is the source; let our fountains burst.
Rivers of water will reach far and wide.
There's a steady flow of life; in Jesus, we abide.
Hear and heed to whatever the Lord tells us to do.
Believe and on Him rely; the way of the world subdue.

Fountains of Graciousness

"But whosoever drinketh of the water that I shall give him shall never thirst; but the water that I shall give him shall be in him a well of water springing up into everlasting life."

JOHN 4:14

The River of Life is a constant flow.
There is blessing along the way as on His path we go.
To Jesus Christ we will be true.
The source of the power, O Lord, is from You.
Drink from His well and never thirst.
A constant flowing from Him will burst.
The Holy Spirit releases the Word, expressible.
The flow of water is irrepressible.
Flow from His source is steady and sure.
We are personally blessed when the water is pure.

Make us ever ready.
May the flow of love be steady.
The power of God is of sweet essence.
What an awesome joy to be in His presence.
Oh Lord, may we become living waterways.
May we be filled with love, joy and praise.
A channel of blessing we are made to be.
Lives are touched and souls are set free.
To live forever in His kingdom is our desire.
God's blessings are abundant;
He is the great supplier.

Choose What is Right

"Casting down imaginations, and every high thing
that exalteth itself against the knowledge of God, and
bringing into captivity every thought to the obedience
of Christ."

II CORINTHIANS 10:5

Selfish yearnings are abolished.
Through divine strength, sin is demolished.
Worldly quests must be erased.
God's love and power are embraced.
With worldly pleasures, make no compromise.
True morality, on the Spirit, relies.
May all our thoughts with Christ be in one accord.
Life and peace prevail; Jesus is Lord!
Spreading the Gospel is our spiritual assignment.
Bring every thought into Christ's alignment.

On this we insist:
The devil, we resist!
How can we, by God, best be used?
To live for His glory, evil is refused.
With heavenly thoughts one must associate.
Never with the devil negotiate.
Our Lord knows what is best.
In Him, we find rest.
Moral choices are proper, when we walk in the light.
Draw upon God's power within and do what is right.

Saved to Serve

"Casting down imaginations, and every high thing
that exalteth itself against the knowledge of God, and
bringing into captivity every thought to the obedience
of Christ:"

II CORINTHIANS 10:5

Our thoughts are captive; to Christ, we will yield.
The Word is our sword and our shield.
Christ has taught us to obey.
Do the Father's will each day.
By the Lord's life, we are led.
Not my way, but His instead.
We are in a spiritual battle.
Keep your lips from idle prattle.
Arguments or pretension against
God are demolished.
When we overcome, those things are abolished.

In every project,
To Christ, be subject.
Thoughts of helpfulness, He does instill.
He plants them in us; go forth and fulfill.
May Christ captivate each thought.
It is then we will do the things we ought.
We will fight the enemy of reason.
The Lord equips us in each season.
The Lord practices righteousness; in Him, we boast.
He knows us personally; we love Him the most.

Preaching Requires Spiritual Weapons

"Nathaniel saith unto Him, 'Whence knowest thou
me?' Jesus answered and said unto him, 'Before that
Philip called thee, when thou wast under the fig tree I
saw thee.'"

JOHN 1:48

In the workshop of life, we will worship.
Moment by moment, He is Captain of the ship.
Spiritual fitness is a must.
Worship the Lord; in Him, put your trust.
Eternity, with Him, is our destination.
When He calls, we will rise to the occasion.
Crisis reveals our true nature.
Oh, may we, in Christ, become mature.
Worship the Lord; this is essential.
The grace He gives is providential.

Time alone in His presence is pure.
Faith in Him will be secure.
Our daily talk,
Strengthens our walk.
In the midst of trials, don't relent.
Time spent in prayer is time well spent.
A secret time alone with the Lord
is a worship session.
We give a promising, positive,
inspirational confession.
God provides a secret corner and He meets us there.
He equips us for each trial; He is with us everywhere.

Prepare For Preaching

"If I then, your Lord and Master, have washed your
feet; ye also ought to wash one another's feet."

JOHN 13:14

The Lord commands the work of our hands.
In each situation, He understands.
God's timing is always right.
He leads the way and helps us fight.
Small troubles help us to prepare.
When the big trials come, He is always there.
The Lord has set for us an example.
He is within us and He is ample.
We can meet the crisis with a smile.
With God, we go the second mile.

The Lord has made a sincere request.
Follow His leading; He knows what is best.
If our little deeds seem insignificant,
God can make them magnificent!
What is the Christian's foremost attitude?
It should be one of love and servitude.
It is God's power within that enables us to perform.
Every day situations are an opportunity to transform.
Menial daily tasks are not underrated or depreciated.
Thank the Lord, who keeps us fit; this is appreciated.

The Vital Force in Disorder

"But Jesus answered and said, 'Ye know not what ye ask. Are ye able to drink of the cup that I shall drink of, and to be baptized with the baptism that I am baptized with?' They say unto Him, 'We are able.'"

MATTHEW 20:22

Sometimes His friendship may seem discrete.
In the midst of confusion, we may feel beat.
When God's loving care is not evident,
We know that in Him we can still be confident.
Whatever we ask for,
God is willing to give more.
The born again are faithful, awaiting Christ's return.
For His established kingdom, we all yearn.
Our requests are not neglected.
God's answer differs from what we expected.

All of God's promises are true.
Listen as He speaks to you.
God is never far away.
He knows our thoughts and hears us pray.
Sometimes we are perplexed and confused.
In His time, He answers; He has not refused.
Many times our faith has been tested.
When our faith is sincere, in Him, we have rested.
Keep asking and believing; do not give up.
Keep the faith; see what God's plan will develop.

Communion Forever

"I have glorified Thee on the earth: I have finished
the work which Thou gavest Me to do."

JOHN 17:4

Let my will be God's will,
He will, with the Spirit, fill.
Come to Him with a heart that is yielded.
When we do His will, our lives are shielded.
Jesus is sufficient; He meets the crisis.
In His name, He authorizes.
God does not force, but gently persuades.
We do surrender and won't do escapades.
Surrender for deliverance, devotion and death.
Rest, sufficiency, and communion.
He does bequeath.

We are together forever.
He leaves us never.
Seek His will and wait for instruction.
The Holy Spirit oversees reconstruction.
Believe and follow God's master plan.
He saves, keeps and gives His grace to man.
After a truce, reconstruction begins.
Tasks are fulfilled as the Spirit disciplines.
Communion with God should not be broken.
His delight is our pleasure; His great love has spoken.

Forming Communicating Ideas

"But I fear, lest by any means, as the serpent beguiled
Eve through his subtilty, so your minds should be
corrupted from the simplicity that is in Christ."

II CORINTHIANS 11:3

God's sincere message will be clear.
Be obedient, when His voice you hear.
Our own kind of thinking may be complex.
Obedience to the Word does not perplex.
To accomplish a task, what is expedient?
Make it plain and be obedient.
My devotion to Christ is sincere and pure.
Guard against evil; by faith, endure.
Don't let your mind be in disorder.
Christ gives victory; He sets our border.

It is expedient,
To be obedient.
Your purpose won't crimple,
When you keep life simple.
Life should be lived without show off veneer,
Live a life that, in Christ, is sincere.
Going our own selfish way may become depressing.
Do what is right and good and be a blessing.
Blindness in our understanding, is the enemy's tool.
Resist what is evil and let the Spirit rule.

Rejection of Falsehood

"But have renounced the hidden things of dishonesty,
not walking in craftiness, nor handling the Word of
God deceitfully; but by manifestation of the truth
commending ourselves to every man's conscience in
the sight of God."

II CORINTHIANS 4:2

Be ready all evil and worldly ways to renounce.
Honesty and righteousness, gladly announce.
Be ever-watchful of your disposition.
Be not ashamed of your position.
Dishonesty, envy, jealousy and strife,
Do not belong in a Christian's life.
Renounce secret, shameful ways.
Set forth the truth; be full of praise.
Continually watch, that you not be led astray.
Speak the Word openly;
speak His truths day by day.

What we hear from the Lord, we are expected to do.
We are blessed in our deeds and true faith we accrue.
Shameful ways are completely dismissed,
When evil thoughts we will resist.
Expel all the hidden things of shame.
Clearly and completely obey, in Jesus' name.
The Word is our standard; sinful ways annoy.
Moment by moment our lives, in Christ, are full of joy.
Envy, jealousy, and strife are snares of the evil one.
False teaching reject;
God's high standards have won.

The Holy Sphere of Practical Piety

"But thou, when thou prayest, enter into thy closet,
and when thou hast shut thy door, pray to thy Father
which is in secret; and thy Father which seeth in
secret shall reward thee openly."

MATTHEW 6:6

We will pray to our Father in secret.
When we have a problem, we need not fret.
To know the Father is impelling.
Pray, in secret, each burden telling.
Yes, enter the closet and close the door.
It is there requests to God we implore.
The fervent prayer of a righteous one,
According to His will, is done.
When praying, don't use empty words and phrases.
Fill your heart with requests and praises.

May our prayers be heard,
As we pray Your Word.
Let not our prayers become repetitive,
It is then they act as a sedative.
Pray earnestly with the closet door closed,
There the heart's desire is, to God, exposed.
Scripture flows through us to the throne of grace.
Petitions are made and we respond with praise.
Wash yourselves clean; proceed to do what is right.
In God's favor we live and, in Him, we delight.

Is Inducement to Do Evil, Good?

"There hath no temptation taken you but such as is
common to man: but God is faithful, who will not
suffer you to be tempted above that ye are able; but
will with the temptation also make a way to escape,
that ye may be able to bear it."

I CORINTHIANS 10:13

Everyone upon this earth is tempted.
On God's highest ground, sin is exempted.
God lifts us up to a higher plane,
When we do not murmur or complain.
To be tempted is not sin.
Victory stems from faith within.
Christ gives us the strength and grace to resist.
Trust fully in Him; He will assist.
A way out of temptation, the Lord does provide.
Refuse all evil; His support is at our side.

We are all enticed and tempted and tested.
God gives us the help we have requested.
Inducement to evil comes to all.
Don't allow sinfulness to appall.
Every human being is, by sin, enticed.
When tested, we will trust and Christ has sufficed.
God made reconciliation for
the sins of the human race.
We deserve condemnation, but Jesus took our place.
When in difficulty we may not know what to do.
Christ directs our moral direction, faith to renew.

Victorious, Most Glorious

"For we have not an High Priest which cannot be touched with the feeling of our infirmities; but was in all points tempted like as we are, yet without sin."

HEBREWS 4:15

Jesus was in all points tempted.
He feels our infirmities; from sin we are exempted.
Yield not to temptation; God's grace does soothe.
The enemy tempts us to stray from the truth.
Satan plants doubts and we wonder
what God said.
Victory is ours; trust Christ, instead.
Confidently, we approach His throne.
He has called us to be His own.
Jesus has compassion; He does understand.
He's been through it all and will hold our hand.

Let not your goals be shifted.
By the Lord's mercy, be lifted.
When we are tempted, He meets our needs.
The enemy entices; the Lord impedes.
Our High Priest, Jesus, for us has sympathy.
He also was tempted and has great empathy.
The home we have in heaven is very appealing.
A wonderful future is in store through His healing.
Our High Priest is Jesus; mercy He bestows.
Draw near to the Lord, where forgiveness flows.

We Trust and Jesus Accomplishes

"Ye are they which have continued with
Me in My temptations."

LUKE 22:28

We must walk with Jesus all the way.
He leads and guides each step, day by day.
The world, the flesh and devil will entice.
Through each temptation, Christ will suffice.
Jesus never fails; He will see us through.
He perseveres; He makes all things new.
Be ready to go where the Lord leads.
When temptation comes, He intercedes.
The Lord Jesus graciously keeps on giving,
So, an abundant life, we keep living.

We hear, obey and share;
God blesses everywhere!
In whatever God has permitted,
We must be fully committed.
Our trial is really Jesus' trial.
Trust Him; make no denial.
Through afflictions in life, we can continue.
Remember always that the Spirit is within you.
Believe and trust our Lord and Savior.
He directs our course and corrects our behavior.

Perfection is the Rule in God's School

"Be ye therefore perfect, even as your Father which is
in heaven is perfect."

MATTHEW 5:48

God's love shows no partiality.
His perfect love is a reality.
To all men be not greedy.
Share what you have with the needy.
At His table come and dine.
Our rule for living is now divine.
He cleanses, renews and enables us to obey.
We are dedicated to Him from day to day.
Through our actions, God's love is voiced.
In the midst of a conflict, we can be poised.

May the love of Christ be made known,
As our love, to others, is shown.
In Christ, we are complete.
We no longer, with the world, compete.
Complete in Christ, Who is the Way.
We grow more like Him day by day.
We trust not in ourselves, but rely on His grace.
In Christ be complete and His mercy embrace.
Vengeance is the Lord's; evil, He will repay.
Enjoy God's grace and salvation
and be quick to obey.

God's Purpose is Our Mission

"And now, saith the LORD that formed me from the
womb to be His servant, to bring Jacob again to Him,
'Though Israel be not gathered, yet shall I be glorious
in the eyes of the LORD, and my God shall be my
strength.'"

ISAIAH 49:5

All for God's glory, is our reason for living.
He bestows His love and keeps on giving.
For God's purpose, we will attend.
His love is genuine; we will not pretend.
We are servants of God's design.
Because of His sacrifice, our lives He does refine.
We are created for God; He made you and me.
May He be glorified as we live in victory.
We must bring His message to all nations.
Bring glory to Him and tend to your stations.

A Christian is formed to be a servant.
Bring Him glory; be more fervent.
Those who promote good, love their Master.
He meets our needs in each disaster.
The love of God, through us, He shares.
On the cross, Christ proved He cares.
The love a Christian gives to the Lord is significant.
God gets the glory and He is magnificent.
Today is the day of salvation;
it is a day of God's favor.
The Shepherd will feed us and He makes us braver.

We Minister; He Holds our Hand

"Ye call Me Master and Lord: and ye say well;
for so I am."

JOHN 13:13

God will save us from disaster.
Jesus is our Lord and Master.
Our Lord heads our household.
He makes it a stronghold.
Our Master is Christ, the Son.
In complete obedience, the battle is won.
He saves, sanctifies and heals, His love to reveal.
Yield your heart to Him; His power is real.
What do we, of the Lord, expect.
We will obey; He will direct.

In His presence, we do bask.
He enables us for each task.
Our Master is forever near.
His voice we respond to, as we hear.
As servants of Christ, to Him, we belong.
He is our breath and our life; He fills us with song.
As children of God, we want to please the Father.
Step by step we walk and work;
to comply is no bother.
People God sends have an appointed mission.
When God speaks to our hearts; we obey the vision.

The Goal is God's Glory

"Then He took unto Him the twelve, and said unto
them, 'Behold, we go up to Jerusalem, and all things
that are written by the prophets concerning the Son of
man shall be accomplished.'"

LUKE 18:31

To do God's will is our constant goal.
We will trust in Him, for He makes us whole.
The will of God led Christ to the cross.
He reached His destination without a loss.
The aim of a missionary is to do
what God commands.
There's a purpose for us; we are safe in His hands.
May Christ prevail from the start.
We will never, ever part.
When doing what God wants, be not discouraged.
With your eyes on the Lord, you'll be encouraged.

Our Savior leads us all the way,
In what to do and what to say.
We do not need to walk alone.
We proceed down the path He has shown.
With Christ we start; with Christ we end.
The road leads to glory; He is our Friend.
For this reason, Christ, the Son, came.
We are cleansed by the blood in Jesus' name.
Grace and mercy has supplied us in our need.
He took away our sin and continues to intercede.

Reconcile; Then Get Ready

"Therefore if thou bring thy gift to the altar, and there
rememberest that thy brother hath
ought against thee;"

MATTHEW 5:23

We are not our own. We must with others share.
God convicts of our sin and helps us to prepare.
Secrets, big and small, from God cannot be hid.
Confess, forsake, repent; of every sin be rid.
It is the little things that count.
With His marvelous grace, God does surmount.
The Holy Spirit will protect.
The slightest sin He will detect.
Our stubborn will is what must break.
Be reconciled; confess it and God's will take.

When the Spirit convicts of sin,
Repent and let His plan begin.
When, with evil, you are involved,
With the Lord, it must be absolved.
The Holy Spirit sees a fault and convicts.
Repent from each sin that He depicts.
The Word of God prepares us for the examination.
We will aim for the goal; that is our exclamation.
Make peace with your brother on the way to the altar.
There should be no grudges that cause us to falter.

September 25

Our Mission is His Commission

"And whosoever shall compel thee to go a mile, go
with him twain."

MATTHEW 5:41

The work is before us; God supplies the power.
His supernatural love is ours this hour.
We ask Him what He would have us to do.
To His will alone we will be true.
The Lord will guide us when we submit to His will.
His own love He does instill.
He helps us to go the second mile.
We can meet each challenge with a smile.
Jesus gave the Sermon on the Mount.
He enables; come to the fount.

When we hear Him tell us to go,
He will go with us, we know.
Do more than what is expected.
Kind deeds are, by the Lord, perfected.
God sends us forth, sometimes beyond our borders.
Expect to receive because He gives perfect orders.
Remember what is honest and
proper and live in peace.
Show kindness and seek goodness;
your fears will cease.
Believe and do His will, His glory to exemplify.
Our time upon the earth quickly passes by.

The Father's Enduring Love   Page 284

Uncensored Disposition

"Leave there thy gift before the altar, and go thy way;
first be reconciled to thy brother, and then come and
offer thy gift."

MATTHEW 5:24

Mend broken hearts with your sister and brother.
God's prerequisite is to love one another.
Our attitude must not be bitter.
Confess and forsake; be not a quitter.
We do not stand up for selfish rights,
Upon the Lord, we set our sights.
When, at the alter, you are convicted,
Go, right the wrong that has been inflicted.
Faithful are we when we mend each wrong.
How sweet it is; to Christ we belong.

When the Spirit, your heart, has convicted of sin,
Repent and let His divine plan begin.
When, with sin, you are offended.
Repent; God's mercy is extended.
Be not by other's faults defiled.
Go to them and be reconciled.
God can turn strife into a thing of beauty.
Restore friendship; that is our duty.
As consecrated people of God,
in Christ we will remain.
Immorality is looked upon with disdain.

Rejecting Our Objecting

"And it came to pass, that, as they went in the way,
a certain man said unto Him, 'Lord, I will follow thee
whithersoever thou goest.'"

LUKE 9:57

God knows what is in man's heart.
The Holy Spirit convicts; guidance He does impart.
Yes, our Lord knows what is in the heart of man.
Deceitfulness does not fit in His plan.
Lord, we will follow You wherever You go.
Feelings are hurt; there are things we should know.
Put your hand to the plow and don't look back.
He gives strength and mercy; in Him is no lack.
When He calls, continue on His path.
He will strengthen you and save from wrath.

To follow Christ, self is denied.
Go with Him; in Him abide.
We tell the Lord that we are ready.
We need His Word; we read it steady.
Renounce the errors of past days.
Refuse to live in carnal ways.
On the cross Jesus endured our pain.
Day by day, in Christ we remain.
Jesus came to save us from the penalty of death.
Publish good tidings; let His praise be on your breath.

Follow Him without Reservation

"Then Jesus beholding him loved him, and said unto
him, 'One thing thou lackest: go thy way, sell
whatsoever thou hast, and give to the poor, and thou
shalt have treasure in heaven: and come, take up the
cross and follow Me.'"

MARK 10:21

To Jesus, our Lord, we surrender all.
He lifts us up so we will not fall.
Take up His cross and be set free.
Identify with Him now and eternally.
Life is rewarding when, with Christ, we are united.
To be transformed by Him, we are delighted.
To follow Christ will be our passion.
Nothing compares to His compassion.
No more, in the paths of sin, do we wallow.
Only Jesus will we follow.

God, from fearful to victorious, changes lives,
When, to His bidding, faith survives
From worldly ways, He will disenchant.
God transforms; we are triumphant.
There is no greater entity,
Than to be in Christ's identity.
Every social contact should be Christ-related.
Jesus is Lord and this is firmly stated.
The stony heart is no longer;
a new heart is put in place.
The Spirit, within, causes us to walk in His ways.

Mentally Awake to God's Summons

"For though I preach the Gospel, I have nothing to
glory of: for necessity is laid upon me; yea, woe is
unto me, if I preach not the Gospel!"

I CORINTHIANS 9:16

We are winners; we cannot lose.
The path of God, we faithfully choose.
To preach the Word is a necessity when called.
We don't hold back, we are enthralled.
To be sanctified is to be set apart.
Love the Lord with all your heart.
We are compelled to preach the Good News.
He has chosen us; His own life He endues.
We have been chosen; this, the Lord has spoken.
Our own selfish plans are then broken.

It is the Lord, alone, we want to please.
We abide in His love; He puts us at ease.
God has ordained us for His pleasure.
His very presence is our treasure.
The call of God is constant and steady.
We hear His pleading; we are ready.
With the Master's call, we are very much aware.
We have a love in our hearts
and a willingness to share.
The many blessings of God's favor, we will not omit.
We preach the Gospel and all the joy that goes with it.

Performing Our Duty

"Who now rejoice in my sufferings for you, and fill up
that which is behind of the afflictions of Christ in my
flesh for His body's sake, which is the Church:"

COLOSSIANS 1:24

Squeezed grapes make sweet wine.
The Lord, alone, can our lives refine.
Sometimes God may put us in a peculiar place.
It is there He helps us win the race.
To God's desires we will adjust.
Fully, in Him, we will trust.
To the lost, the Gospel preach.
Christ enables us to teach.
In Christ's sufferings, we will share.
He sends His comfort everywhere.

The Lord sends us on a mission.
Preach the Word; it is His commission.
May this fact be clearly stated:
In Christ, we are saved and emancipated.
Our possessions do not matter.
Full commitment makes us gladder.
Don't expect to always live a life of ease.
Sometimes the Lord must give a tight squeeze.
Wisdom is one of God's attributes.
As we seek His direction, He contributes.

October

*Put ye in the sickle, for the harvest is ripe:
come, get you down; for the press is full, the
fats overflow; for their wickedness is great.
Multitudes, multitudes in the valley of decision:
for the day of the LORD is near in the valley of
decision. Joel 3:13, 14*

The Influential Prompting of the Spirit

"And after six days Jesus taketh with Him Peter, and James, and John, and leadeth them up into an high mountain apart by themselves: and He was transfigured before them."

MARK 9:2

To the Mount, we sometimes ascend,
But back to the valley, we descend.
The world and cares oftentimes discourage.
In God we trust; He gives us courage.
It is great when earthly cares are halted.
As we praise the Lord, He is exalted.
He was transfigured in the disciple's presence.
Encourage, announce and endorse,
in sweet essence.
Alone, with our Savior and Lord, we are set apart.
It is then, new insight He does impart.

We drink deeply from the well.
When we are filled, God instructs us to go and tell.
At the mountain top, we see afar.
It is a time apart from the regular.
Moments on the mount are for inspiration.
The fresh breath He gives is an aspiration.
What a glorious view, when the whole picture we see.
It is refreshing and it equips us for the valley.
Jesus only is to be listened to and constantly obeyed.
Prayers are answered to the pleas we have made.

The Influence of the Lowly

"And ofttimes it hath cast him into the fire, and into the waters, to destroy him: but if thou canst do anything, have compassion on us, and help us."

MARK 9:22

From the mountaintop, we exalt.
May our praises to God never halt.
Down in the valley, we are freed from pride.
We will live for His glory; in Him, we abide.
In the valley of humiliation, we find God's worth.
Doubt and unbelief don't belong to
those of new birth.
Wherever we are, we will live for His glory.
It is in Christ that we can claim victory.
To know the Lord is to love Him and do His will.
His power makes us whole; His love does fulfill.

We all have our ups and downs.
Hopelessness, we will renounce.
We make plans, but God has something better.
His way is perfect; trust Him to unfetter.
On mountaintops, we dream of mighty acts.
Back in the valley, we face the facts.
From highest peaks to the valley below,
Jesus loves and cares for us; this we really know.
All things are possible to those who believe.
He lifts up the fallen; to Him we will cleave.

The Influence of Performing Service

"And He said unto them, this kind can come forth by nothing, but by prayer and fasting."

MARK 9:29

Obey God and it will please.
His wondrous mercies never cease.
Lord, we want to know You more.
Be our exclusive Counselor.
With the Lord, we are acquainted.
Through each trial, we have not fainted.
When there is little faith, there is little prayer.
It is then that chaos reigns everywhere.
Trials may be heavy and doubt foreseen,
Rest in His mercy; let nothing come between.

For Him, alone, is what we yearn.
We sit at His feet and there we learn.
When it is Jesus we know,
In faith, we will grow.
To serve the Lord, sit at His table.
To know Him is to love Him and He alone is able.
By the world, be not distracted.
To the Lord, we must be attracted.
By prayer and fasting many desires are satisfied.
Ask according to God's will; we will not be denied.

The Foresight and the Reality

"Unto the Church of God which is at Corinth, to them
that are sanctified in Christ Jesus, called to be saints,
with all that in every place call upon the name of
Jesus Christ our Lord, both theirs and ours:"

I CORINTHIANS 1:2

God has called us with a vision.
His command is our commission.
God has a part in each commonplace event.
Time enveloped in His Word is time well spent.
With His vision before us, we run the race.
Thank the Lord for each valley we face.
Holiness is real to those who belong.
We're called to be saints and He fills us with song.
He makes known His will in our training.
Let Him not find us complaining.

Walk in the light of His vision.
Obedience to His calling is our mission.
Saints are believers.
They are Christ receivers.
Be obedient to His vision; do not be depressed.
Bumps and bruises come;
may God's love be expressed.
God has revealed to us what we can become.
There are many saints in Christendom.
Joyfulness and righteousness are God's attributes.
Know the Lord; His grace and mercy He contributes.

The Influence of Low Moral Standards

"Wherefore, as by one man sin entered into the world,
and death by sin; and so death passed upon all men,
for that all have sinned:"

ROMANS 5:12

Our immoral nature is crucified.
On Christ's disposition, we have relied.
Sin, in man, is our earthly disposition.
In Christ, we receive a new position.
All have sinned and fallen short.
Be born again is God's retort.
Sin entered the world through one man.
Christ came to redeem; that is God's plan.
Every human, to death is subject.
Our Redeemer came to bring life and not to reject.

By sin we are degenerated.
By Christ we are regenerated.
To God's likeness we are restored.
We say thank You to the Lord.
All have sinned and have missed God's glory.
Redeemed through Christ; that is the Gospel story.
The choice is ours; which will it be?
Redemption, in Christ, sets us free.
Let us live in harmony and
let us not dwell on the past.
Love is sincere; loathe evil and to the good hold fast.

Spiritual Renewal

"But when it pleased God, who separated me from my
mother's womb, and called me by His grace, to reveal
His Son in me, that I might preach Him among the
heathen; immediately I conferred not
with flesh and blood:"

GALATIANS 1:15-16

The answer to despair is to be in Christ.
On the cross, our Savior was sacrificed.
In Christ, our life has been renewed.
His hatred of sin is also our attitude.
Make us new is our humble plea.
He gives His life that we may be set free.
He's revealed His Son; let us proclaim:
We are saved, healed and sanctified in Jesus name.
We are with God and for God set apart.
We love the Lord with all our heart.

Temptations play a beckoning part.
We need not heed when Christ is in the heart.
Purity and holiness avails; faith in Christ is confessed.
We are renewed in the Spirit and abundantly blessed.
God is love; we have holy boldness, evil to defy.
Be conformed to His image; He does sanctify.
Jesus is the Anointed One; He gives new life.
The Author of salvation gives grace, not strife.
The Lord is our Helper; we will not be alarmed.
Trust and be confident we will not be harmed.

Restored to Friendship

"For He hath made Him to be sin for us, who knew no sin; that we might be made the righteousness of God in Him."

II CORINTHIANS 5: 21

Sin, in man, is inherited.
Full salvation, Christ has merited.
God hates sin; Christ paid the price.
He obediently became the sacrifice.
God has made of the sinner a saint.
We'll walk in His ways and will not faint.
Christ became an offering for us upon the cross.
We are made righteous; He takes away dross.
In Christ, we have become a new creation.
Remain in the union of reconciliation.

Be as lights in a dark place.
Christ's true nature, you can embrace.
To the Lord, we give our all.
When we trust Him, we will not fall.
We really want to avoid disaster.
We must make the Lord our Master.
Our lives, through Christ, are set free and rearranged.
Sin is blotted out;
we are no longer from God estranged.
Christ's love is everlasting; He will not discourage.
Have confidence in the Lord;
He gives hopeful courage.

The Significant Savior

"Come unto Me, all ye that labour and are heavy laden, and I will give you rest."

MATTHEW 11: 28

We come to Jesus, just as we are, this hour.
He fulfills us with His power.
All He asks us to do is to come to Him and rest.
He defeated the enemy with a mighty conquest.
Though the burden He bared is not light,
Know that He will ease our pain with His great might.
Our days should not be wearisome.
The Lord helps us to overcome.
Come to Jesus; we are invited.
Accept His call; in Him be excited.

When we heed to His call,
He sends us on our missions.
When we obey, God opens His provisions.
The call to come to Jesus is directly indicated.
Because of Him, our lives are justified, yes vindicated.
We're not overburdened; our souls are refreshed.
Worldly ties are broken; we are no longer enmeshed.
Each waking moment, God's message we promote.
We run the race with joy and our lives to God devote.
We are children of God; our lives He does enhance.
We are changed into His resemblance.

Accept the Atonement

"Neither yield ye your members as instruments of unrighteousness unto sin: but yield yourselves unto God, as those that are alive from the dead, and your members as instruments of righteousness unto God."

ROMANS 6:13

To Christ's righteousness and holiness yield.
Work as a laborer in His field.
On Christ's atoning work we must rely.
Only He, alone, can sanctify.
Have faith in what Jesus Christ has done.
We are redeemed through the blood of the Son.
Our obedience is the Lord's delight.
He puts fears and doubts to flight.
Humans, in natural self, are very weak.
The atonement of grace we seek.

He upholds us in each fight.
Draw from His great strength and might.
Grace and mercy walk together.
Our tendency to do wrong, He will tether.
God makes of us instruments to do right.
Become one with Him and spread His Light.
With Christ, we are as one.
Sin and evil, we will shun.
When living under grace, sin will not dominate.
We are set free; God's purpose will predominate.

How Do We Express Our Awareness?

"At that time Jesus answered and said, 'I thank Thee, O Father, Lord of heaven and earth, because Thou hast hid these things from the wise and prudent, and hast revealed them unto babes.'"

MATTHEW 11:25

We walk in His light when we obey.
The Spirit leads each step of the way.
God's plan unfolds; trust Him each day.
Press on toward the goal; don't delay.
He has cleansed us from all sin.
We are born again, Christ lives within.
His hidden secrets are withheld from the proud.
To the humble, His wisdom will be endowed.
When you trust Him, the light will shine.
You can proceed on His path, divine.

Obey!
Don't stray!
We are elated.
To Christ, we are related.
Receive the Word with joy; Jesus never fails.
In Him we are more than conquerors; victory avails.
Oh Lord, may our relationship be daily perfected.
We are established in love;
spiritual growth is affected.
Walk down in the guided path; it is there we find rest.
The Lord refreshes our soul; He does what is best.

Rest; then Expect

"When He had heard therefore that he was sick, He
abode two days still in the same place
where He was."

JOHN 11:6

Like the rest in music, God's silence is song.
It is part of the composition and moves right along.
God sometimes answers prayers with silence.
In the midst of it, He proves His excellence.
God's quietness is not demeaning.
His fields are ready for gleaning.
Keep on trusting as, on Him, you wait.
The answers to prayer are blessing, not fate.
According to God's wisdom, He answers prayer.
Just remember, He is always there.

When His perfect will we seek,
He whispers peace and then He will speak.
Silence and calm,
Could be God's healing balm.
In the midst of God's hush, He speaks of His glory.
The events that occur are totally explanatory.
Be still and know that God is near.
Our quiet requests He will hear.
As we walk in the daytime, we will walk in the light.
Trust in the Lord; on Him rely and do what is right.

Walk and talk with the Lord

"And Enoch walked with God: and he was not; for
God took him."

GENESIS 5:24

Side by side and in God's stride.
We will walk and, in Christ, abide.
From His pathway we will not stray
When He leads, we will obey.
Come, walk with Him and be revived.
In His steps, we have survived.
Day by day, He will encourage.
Our hopes are in Him; He will not discourage.
Don't stop in your tracks; keep moving on.
Be trained and disciplined by the Son.

With God, we walk.
With God, we talk.
Take one step at a time
Be in His presence, sublime.
Learn to see from the Father's standpoint.
In ordinary things, He does appoint.
The Spirit and the sinful nature are in conflict.
Keep in step with the Spirit; the enemy, contradict.
May our fellowship with God be steady and habitual.
Praises from the heart are sincere
and not just a ritual.

Train, then Gain

"Then saith He unto His disciples, 'The harvest truly is
plenteous, but the labourers are few;"

MATTHEW 9:37

Who am I that I should go?
Teach and train me; then, I'll know.
Communion with God takes first place,
If we are to run and win the race.
The Lord will send us on a mission,
But first of all, we need a vision.
God, the Father, with Jesus is pleased.
He redeems the sinful and heals the diseased.
Training may take many years.
The great I AM dispels our fears.

Our reaction
Should be God's action.
When one with God, the Son,
The battle is sure to be won.
Spend your time in studying God's Word.
To win souls, the Gospel message must be heard.
Many hours are spent on God's training ground.
He teaches us lessons that are profound.
We must learn to listen and open our hearts wide.
This is accomplished when, in Christ, we abide.

Impelled to Witness

"Verily, verily, I say unto you, He that believeth on
Me, the works that I do shall he do also; and greater
works than these shall he do; because I go unto My
Father."

JOHN 14:12

God commands us to go and teach.
There are so many souls to reach.
The Lord endues us with His power.
We may manifest His life this hour.
All power is given unto Christ.
Abide in Him; He has sufficed.
We will not be disappointed,
If we go where He's appointed.
He tells us we must, the Gospel, propagate.
Reach out to others; in love, participate.

We are asked to preach in God's authority.
We're appointed; the task is mandatory.
To make disciples, He does command.
With new life in Christ, we understand.
To go means simply to live and let His light shine.
Our desire is to give each and every time.
The Lord is absolutely sovereign and supreme.
Witness in all places; defeat the devil's scheme.
The love of God in the life of a Christian is evident.
In the midst of disaster, we see that God is provident.

The Vital Message of Salvation

"And He is the propitiation for our sins: and not for ours only, but also for the sins of the whole world."

I JOHN 2:2

The Lamb of God cleanses from sin.
Christ redeems; ask Him to come in.
The missionary message knows no limit.
It has no power without Him in it.
The Holy Ghost brings us, with Christ, in union.
There is no better sweet communion.
God's righteousness has been satisfied.
Christ took the punishment; for us, He died.
Forgiveness is given to those who repent.
To sinful deeds, we will relent.

The Lamb of God we share.
Go spread His message everywhere.
The shed blood of the Lamb takes away our sin.
Believe, repent; ask Christ within.
Jesus took upon Himself the
punishment for our sins.
When we repent and receive Him new life begins.
God's Word is the Gospel to share with the world.
Christ is our protector from evil darts that are hurled.
Keep the treasures of the Word and, in Him, abide.
Love not worldly ways; in God's presence reside.

Our Director's Commands

"Pray ye therefore the Lord of the harvest, that He
will send forth labourers into His harvest."

MATTHEW 9:38

The harvest fields are waiting.
God requests that there be no hesitating.
The entire world is God's field.
He tells us to go and, to His Spirit, yield.
The first step on a mission is prayer.
God owns the harvest everywhere.
Let the love of Jesus flow through you.
In the harvest field, there is work to do.
Be not bogged down with selfish ways.
Be ready to sing and give the Lord praise.

He fills us with knowledge,
When Him, we acknowledge.
We are called to be Jesus' very own.
It is then we make His presence known.
Not I, but Christ, is on the forefront.
His sword is sharp; without Him, ours is blunt.
Christ is the chief engineer on the job.
He maneuvers circumstances to overcome the mob.
Touch the hem of His garment; be perfectly restored.
What a blessing it is to put our trust in the Lord.

Mighty Accomplishments

"Verily, verily, I say unto you, He that believeth on
Me, the works that I do shall he do also; and greater
works than these shall he do; because I go
unto My Father."

JOHN 14:12

As we pray, God bestows His grace.
As His children, He helps us, each battle to face.
Prayer is called the greater work.
Lord, we want to pray and not to shirk.
Pray whenever and wherever you are.
He will send angels near and far.
In the midst of the battle, pray.
The Lord guides; follow His way.
By prayer, the fruit remains.
God will bless; the kingdom gains.

The seeds must scatter.
Our prayers always matter.
Prayer is vital.
King is His title.
For the greater work, prayer is the key.
It is then that we can walk in victory.
Jesus was sent into the world by the Father.
We go out to witness; we go in faith; it is no bother.
Because Jesus is alive, we shall also live.
He makes Himself real to us; He's regenerative.

Sending Out Support

"Because that for His name's sake they went forth,
taking nothing of the Gentiles."

III JOHN 7

A shepherd's job is to watch and keep.
The Lord has told us to feed His sheep.
Through the Christian, His love is manifest.
We rest in Him, for He knows what is best.
May each Christian live a life of truth.
For His sake, serve old, middle-aged and youth.
Work together, the Gospel to spread.
Lift up His name and don't be misled.
For His name's sake, we march ahead.
Go not in the world's way, but Christ's way instead.

To the Lord, we are attached,
So others, to Him, may be matched.
There is only one goal.
It is to save the soul.
We are in the world, but not of it.
We go in His name; there is no name above it.
The nature of the Lord Jesus Christ is the key.
He helps us to live lives of victory.
Let us not imitate evil, but let us do what is right.
Walk in the Spirit and in Jesus delight.

Attentive Enlightenment

"Jesus answered, 'My kingdom is not of this world: if
My kingdom were of this world, then would My
servants fight, that I should not be delivered to the
Jews: but now is My kingdom not from hence.'"

JOHN 18:36

We do not work for the praises of men.
We need not announce the where and the when.
Time, alone with God, is well-spent.
Count on His enlightenment.
The kingdom of God is perfectly pure.
He helps the weakest saint to endure.
God's kingdom is righteousness, peace, and joy.
His grace and mercy, He does employ.
It is great to know the Lord in person.
He is always our Friend, though trials may worsen.

The kingdom of God is our goal.
Feast on His Word; nourish your soul.
In the Word of God, immerse.
Absorb it, verse by verse.
The truth of God's Word must be dominant.
It is then that the witness will be prominent.
We work and we actively worship with others.
Daily share His Word with all sisters and brothers.
Each one who is of the truth, His voice does hear.
Listen intently; the Message we embrace and endear.

Pure and Free From Sinful Ways

"For this is the will of God, even your sanctification,
that ye should abstain from fornication:"

I THESSALONIANS 4:3

Unto You, oh Lord, have we cried.
In You we are sanctified.
Let God's will be our will.
His life, He will instill.
Pray, serve, and be obedient.
Sanctification is expedient.
It is important to be set apart.
Love the Lord with all your heart.
Let the light of Jesus shine.
Serve and obey the Lord, divine.

May our will be God's will.
It is then, our hearts, He can fill.
To be holy,
Trust God, wholly.
Moment by moment,
In Christ, we are confident.
As we walk in the Spirit, we make many reparations.
From the love of God, there are no separations.
Be zealous followers of that which is good.
Oppose what is evil and do what you should.

Guidance, With Discretion

"But ye, beloved, building up yourselves on your most
holy faith, praying in the Holy Ghost,"

JUDE 20

Discipline yourself to do God's will.
Every need, He can fulfill.
Train impulse into spiritual leading.
The call of God is a gentle pleading.
To the Gospel truth be loyal.
Crown Him King; He is most royal.
To be built up in the faith, we must be trained.
The Spirit has inspired, guided and sustained.
Study the Word and know its teaching.
Know that the Lord, to us, is reaching.

Our motives are strong,
To Christ, we belong.
Our thoughts and deeds can be impulsive.
We could tend to be repulsive.
On this we need to be insistent:
Our walk with the Lord will be consistent.
Observe God's ways from the Word and learn.
What is right and good, we will discern.
Be careful what you hear and read.
It is the Word of God that we really need.

Affirming God's Vital Force

"The Spirit itself beareth witness with our spirit, that
we are the children of God:"

ROMANS 8:16

Children of God need spiritual fitness.
When we come to Him, we will have the witness.
The Spirit nurtures and attests to our spirit.
Come to Jesus; heed His call; hear it.
We are in God's family, the Spirit testifies.
The Word is His truth; the Father never lies.
The Father's love is evident.
Of this, we can be confident.
We want to become spiritually mature.
Take heed to our Lord's divine nature.

We cannot be self-centered pretenders.
A true believer fully surrenders.
The blessings of the Lord, He does entitle.
Our renewed spirit is strong and vital.
The Spirit intercedes and the Father agrees.
He knows our needs and responds to our pleas.
Express the truth; false teaching we will reject.
Holy living the Lord will expect.
Christ Jesus humbled Himself; He is our example.
He has given us His grace and this is ample.

Old Things Are Gone

"Therefore if any man be in Christ, he is a new
creature: old things are passed away; behold, all
things are become new."

II CORINTHIANS 5:17

Our prejudices, God will erase,
Ask His forgiveness before we meet
Him face to face.
Have respect for all; don't be a pretender.
It is to the Lord that we surrender.
All things are of God is our attitude.
He fills our thoughts with praise and gratitude.
In Christ, we are a new creation.
We are born anew is our proclamation.
Be honest; in God, we place our trust.
Complete surrender is a must.

We will not be harassed.
Our old life is past.
With Christ within,
We are able to refrain from sin.
God wants us to give our all.
He will help us; we need not fall.
In Christ, we are made completely new.
We will yield to Him in all we do.
Abiding in Christ determines what is admired.
According to His will, He gives what is desired.

Christ is Victory

"Now thanks be unto God, which always causeth us
to triumph in Christ, and maketh manifest the savour
of His knowledge by us in every place."

II CORINTHIANS 2:14

We are on the winning side.
Our point of view will not be pride.
Seated in the heavenlies, with Him we reign.
We are more than conquerors; in Him we gain.
In triumphal victory, we are led,
By Christ, the victor, we are fed.
Thanks be to God; He is always the winner.
His re-creation makes a saint of a sinner.
In the vastness of Christ's triumphs, we are captive.
For His purpose, we are active.

To conquer, we must in Him abide.
In Jesus, we trust; in Him we hide.
Through Him, we conquer and win the race.
He will see us through each trial we face.
We can always be victorious.
The Lord, our Savior, is most glorious.
The victory has already been won.
We overcome through God, the Son.
We will speak His message and the Gospel relate.
Our motives are pure and no other Word can equate.

The Presence of Circumstances

"To the weak became I as weak, that I might gain the weak: I am made all things to all men, that I might by all means save some."

I CORINTHIANS 9:22

In every situation we have been placed,
God's love, in Christ, is to be embraced.
God has many tasks to do.
Let Him know that He can count on you.
We may be placed in an uncomfortable surrounding.
It is there that God's mighty work is abounding.
Let the Lord have His way in your life.
He will meet your need in the midst of strife.
Where God has put us, is where we should be.
Keep trusting Him, though you may not agree.

Wherever we are placed, we will not relent.
To be in God's hand, is time well-spent.
There are so many people of different races.
Each one is in need of God's embraces.
We will run the race;
of God's presence we are aware.
Tell the Gospel, the blessings we will share.
To walk with the Lord is a sincere delight.
He directs our steps both day and night.
Every good gift is from the Father above.
The greatest gift is the gift of love.

Sent Out By God

"Then said Jesus to them again, Peace be unto you:
as My Father hath sent Me, even so send I you."

JOHN 20:21

In Him, alone, we will take our stand,
We will move at His command.
Go and tell, is His commission,
He has sent us on our mission.
Carry out His plans in a bold attempt.
Those called of God are not exempt.
To the call of Jesus, I'll be true,
Day by day, He will renew.
He has given us His peace.
The joy He gives will never cease.

Do not be discontent.
Know that for His glory, you are sent.
For the Lord, seize the moment.
Live your life in Christ; be confident.
Go forth with the Good News; you are nominated.
The call to the mission field has dominated.
Receive the Holy Spirit, the Lord has proclaimed.
Preach the Gospel of salvation and be not ashamed.
God's calling and His plans are pure.
Be productive when you hear from Him for sure.

The Technique of Preaching the Gospel

"Go ye therefore, and teach all nations, baptizing them in the name of the Father, and of the Son, and of the Holy Ghost:"

MATTHEW 28:19

For our salvation Christ has done the work.
From His call to discipleship, do not shirk.
In Christ, place all your confidence.
He will always rise to our defense.
To the Lord be rightly related.
Go and teach; this is clearly stated.
Remain true to God's call.
Salvation avails for one and all.
For Jesus sake and for our blessing,
We go forth, His Word confessing.

We are selected to tell the Good News.
It is up to the hearers, God's way to choose.
Time alone with God, in prayer, is always special.
We become richer and kinder; make no denial.
Observe what He's commanded; bring no shame.
He is with us always; His glory is our aim.
God's desire must be put into action.
His accomplished tasks bring much satisfaction.
Keep a sound mind; be self-restrained and alert.
Live in the truth; with crooked ways don't flirt.

Excused By Blessing

"For if, when we were enemies, we were reconciled to God by the death of His Son, much more, being reconciled, we shall be saved by His life."

ROMANS 5:10

On the cross, our Savior died.
On this truth, we have relied.
It is all in Jesus, God, the Son.
His sacrificial work is done.
We are daily delivered from sin's dominion.
On the cross it was finished; ask Jesus to come in.
The believer is forgiven; to God, he is reconciled.
We are saved from wrath and no longer defiled.
He paid in full and it is finished.
The grace provided is not diminished.

The sacrifice was made; the work is done.
New life is present in God's Son.
He died, once for all.
On His name, forever call.
It is not by our works or by any merit.
The heavenly kingdom, we gracefully inherit.
In Christ, we have a given joy that will not pass away.
It is just as if we'd never sinned;
we share His life today.
We are justified by Christ's blood;
salvation is for sure.
We are saved; our Savior is righteous and pure.

He Took My Place

"For He hath made Him to be sin for us, who knew no
sin; that we might be made the righteousness
of God in Him."

II CORINTHIANS 5:21

Ask Christ today in your heart to come in.
He can then cleanse your life from every sin.
Jesus was obedient unto death.
He then could, to us, His life bequeath.
We are approved and acceptable in His sight,
When our heart, with Him, is right.
God's righteousness is experienced by the believer.
When one is joined to Christ, that one is a receiver.
Let all the Christians be informed.
Into their lives, Christ is formed.

Our lives are rearranged.
Our sinful life is, through Christ, exchanged.
Always seek to be of God's nature.
It is in Christ, we grow and mature.
Christ takes away our sin's penalty and power.
He paid the price; He is the salvation endower.
Christ is our substitute; we are declared just.
Identification with Him, on the cross, is a must.
Walk onward with the Lord and do not look back.
We know that in the Spirit there is no lack.

Revelation Sense

"But without faith it is impossible to please Him: for
he that cometh to God must believe that He is, and
that He is a rewarder of them
that diligently seek Him."

HEBREWS 11:6

We walk by faith, not by sight.
We trust the Lord with all our might.
Who knows what great things God has planned?
He grants the faith to understand.
To God's children, faith is made real.
His presence and joy has great appeal.
Always put Jesus Christ first.
Faithfully, He will quench our thirst.
To God, we must be rightly related.
To know Him is to love Him; we have joy, elated.

When we have faith, we are certain.
God can move any mountain.
In Christ, we are content and complete.
We no longer, with the world, compete.
We can either be impulsive or inspired.
The Word of God is to be read and admired.
Christians have a given joy that will never pass away.
It is just as if we'd never sinned;
we have His life today.
Our faith is what pleases and satisfies our Jehovah.
Christ is the Morning Star.   We need no other nova.

Understanding God's Revelation

"And Jesus said unto them, 'Because of your unbelief:
for verily I say unto you, If ye have faith as a grain of
mustard seed, ye shall say unto this mountain,
Remove hence to yonder place; and it shall remove;
and nothing shall be impossible unto you.'"

MATTHEW 17:20

Faith cannot be bought or earned.
Through trials and testing, it is learned.
No matter what the circumstance,
Walk by faith and not by chance.
True, effective faith will bring a result.
In Christ, nothing is too difficult.
No matter what happens, in God, we will trust.
When meeting daily trials, faith is a must.
In order for our faith to be exact,
With Christ, we are in direct contact.

All are met with a test,
Those in Christ, can quietly rest.
Faith is the believer's core.
The Word of God provides much more.
We are in the world, but not of it.
We go in His name; there is none above it.
When we are tested, our faith is pure and strong.
It is the hope of our calling; to Him, we belong.
If we meet with contention, we will,
to the Lord, be true.
Divine love and mercy will always see us through.

November

Enter into His gates with thanksgiving, and into His courts with praise: be thankful unto Him, and bless his name. Psalm 100:4

Arise and Shine

"What? Know ye not that your body is the temple of
the Holy Ghost which is in you, which ye have of God,
and ye are not your own?"

I CORINTHIANS 6:19

We are placed on earth to bring God glory.
Don't hinder; proclaim His story.
Someone may face heartbreak today.
Draw near to God; trust His way.
With Christ, we must identify.
Only He can deify.
We have been redeemed, the faithful say.
In the midst of calamity, He shows us the way.
The Lord is with us; arise and shine.
We belong to Him, how supremely divine.

We sometimes go through overpowering sorrow.
His presence makes a brighter tomorrow.
Self is no longer number one.
By grace, live for God, the Son.
For the Gospel, we are set apart each day.
Follow Christ; diligently watch and pray.
We go through hard times to bring us closer to God.
We are called into fellowship and on His path we trod.
We've been bought with Christ's blood on the cross.
Bring glory to God; He has rid us of refuse and dross.

His Orders Set Our Borders

"If ye love Me, keep My commandments."

JOHN 14:15

Choose to obey; the choice is ours.
In the Spirit, be open to pray for hours.
To be His disciple, self, we deny.
As we walk in the Spirit; on Him, we rely.
Love the Lord and be obedient.
Be one with Him; that is expedient.
The Lord tells us what He commands.
The saint, in obedience, on the solid Rock stands.
If you love Him, you will do what you ought.
He makes suggestions, when His will is sought.

A life of love is what we crave.
It is a life of joy; in Him we behave.
We will walk His way,
As we trust and obey.
Heed the choice to accept Him; the Lord says "If,"
When we go our own way, the penalty is stiff.
His standards are sound and very clear.
To follow them, the Word of God endear.
The Comforter has come and He abides forever.
Jesus is made known to us;
His love He will not sever.

Willing and Fulfilling

"I am crucified with Christ: nevertheless I live; yet not
I, but Christ liveth in me: and the life which I now live
in the flesh I live by the faith of the Son of God, who
loved me, and gave Himself for me."

GALATIANS 2:20

To the Lord Jesus Christ, be conformed.
Let Him rule your life; be, by the Spirit, informed.
To self, give away the right.
Follow Him with all your might.
Whatever we do is for Jesus' sake.
Reckon self dead and His nature take.
No longer live by selfish rule.
To live for self is to be a fool.
As we live by faith, we live by the Spirit.
His Word reigns and we revere it.

Christ lives in me; this, we do declare.
His glory abounds everywhere.
Christ is our defender.
Unto Him, we do surrender.
Our love for the Lord is intense and fervent.
To Him, we yield; we can be His bond-servant.
We know not what He will call us to do and be.
Let Him intercept; expectantly, wait and see.
Jesus agrees with the Father's instruction.
Lives are recreated for an amazing production.

His Commands Are Our Demands

"Draw nigh to God, and He will draw nigh to you.
Cleanse your hands, ye sinners; and purify your
hearts, ye double minded."

JAMES 4:8

The call of God demands action.
We hear; we do; that's our reaction.
We willingly perform the task.
He gives far more than we would ask.
Asking Jesus into our heart is vital.
He conducts the mighty recital.
God's nearness indicates His presence.
To our lives, He brings sweet essence.
Draw near to God; respond to His orders.
Do not be enlightened hoarders.

God's Word is exact.
We must react.
When God is near,
We need not fear.
The Lord, we diligently will seek.
He makes us strong when we are weak.
When we act upon our revelation, we are set free.
Step by step we march along in victory.
To God we will be submitted and
He will not neglect us.
When we feel insignificant, He will direct us.

Sharing Through Toleration

"But rejoice, inasmuch as ye are partakers of Christ's
sufferings; that, when His glory shall be revealed, ye
may be glad also with exceeding joy."

I PETER 4:13

In His sufferings, we partake.
May we be used for Jesus' sake.
The trials of suffering can be long.
God makes us fit and keeps us strong.
Do not be amazed at the fiery ordeal.
Through it, His radiance, He will reveal.
We willingly suffer for Christ's cause.
Abundant joy will know no loss.
The love of Jesus will not fail.
We walk with Him upon the trail.

Through our trials, we are refined.
Deliverance comes; keep that in mind.
Seek His knowledge through each test.
For our future, He knows what is best.
Trials and troubles come into our lives.
Show compassion; it is then our faith revives.
Sometimes what happens may seem severe.
The Lord enables us to persevere.
Our personal ambitions can be selfish goals.
He is girding us for battle to win souls.

A Detailed Plan of Full Acceptance

"And whosoever liveth and believeth in Me shall never die. Believest thou this?"

JOHN 11:26

On His Word, we will take our stand.
His desire is our command.
Jesus is the resurrection and the life.
Fret not in unbelief and strife.
Live, believe, have faith; on Him rely,
Peace is what He bestows; He does justify.
Resurrected believers will live forever.
Life is abundant; it's a heaven bound endeavor.
The Word of God reveals the Lord's path.
He sets us free from sin and from eternal wrath.

We can feel the Spirit's tug and pull.
He wants our love for Jesus to be full.
To believe is to commit.
Only Christ, within, makes us fit.
Believing is the prelude to behaving.
Commit to Christ; He does the saving.
With every breath we know that He is there.
We sit at His feet, and rest in His care.
We are glad in the Lord with a joy that far exceeds.
Christ is glorified; He always meets our needs.

Purpose in Your Circumstances

"And we know that all things work together for good to them that love God, to them who are the called according to His purpose."

ROMANS 8:28

The events of our lives are in God's hands.
Pray in the Spirit; He understands.
All things, for believers, work together for good.
The hardest trial can be withstood.
Of this promise we are assured:
When the Spirit prays, His voice is heard.
Friends and family may have a need.
Pray and let the Holy Spirit intercede.
When we are confronted, there is a reason.
For each event in life, there is a season.

Avoid all evil and do what is good.
Heed His commands; every Christian should.
He makes all things work for our well-being.
Joyful assurance and blessings, He is guaranteeing.
In the life of a saint, there is no such thing as chance.
God has His hand in each sacred circumstance.
Our Helper is the Lord; we will not be terrified.
He is our stronghold; His name is glorified.
Only Jesus satisfies the human heart.
From His presence, we will not part.

Intercession, With Confessed Victory

"Likewise the Spirit also helpeth our infirmities: for we
know not what we should pray for as we ought: but
the Spirit itself maketh intercession for us with
groanings which cannot be uttered."

ROMANS 8:26

The power of prayer has no rival.
It is the door to our survival.
In our body, the Holy Spirit resides.
From within, He leads and guides.
The Holy Spirit intercedes.
He knows better what one needs.
It is important that prayer be exercised.
By the Spirit, be energized.
It is difficult for us to find words to express.
The Spirit relieves us of our distress.

From worldly chatter keep your mind clear.
It is then we are able, God's voice to hear.
The Spirit prompts; Christ intercedes.
God, the Father, supplies our needs.
The Father, Son, and Holy Spirit are combined.
May the life of every Christian be refined.
God takes strict notice of each rule we contemplate.
He restrains us from sin; on His Word we meditate.
Prayer is essential in the life of every saint.
God helps us to proceed and not to faint.

Fill My Cup, That I May Serve

"Who now rejoice in my sufferings for you, and fill up
that which is behind of the afflictions of Christ in my
flesh for His body's sake, which is the Church:"

COLOSSIANS 1:24

We will bask in His presence.
He, alone, brings sweet essence.
Proclaim His truth and He will be revealed.
Lift Him up and, to the Spirit, yield.
Our confidence is not in man.
Put your trust in Christ; that is God's plan.
Do not revel in what mortal man can do.
Our lives reveal Christ; we've been born anew.
To Christ, we must be rightly related.
His love and mercy is generated.

The slightest sin, the Spirit detects.
Thank You Lord; Your grace protects.
To reach the lost and lonely,
Lift up Jesus, only.
Live in harmony with Christ and He will amaze.
Great things, through Him,
are wrought through grace.
Christ is exalted; His glorious light shines through us.
Of striking personalities, we will not make a fuss.
Let each generation know they can be emancipated.
May the Word of God be fully known and propagated.

Companionship in Glad Tidings

"And sent Timotheus, our brother, and minister of
God, and our fellow-labourer in the gospel of Christ,
to establish you,
and to comfort you concerning your faith:"

I THESSALONIANS 3:2

In the Lord, be sanctified.
Selfish goals are now denied.
What the Lord wants, should be our aim.
Live for God's purpose and not for fame.
Going one's own selfish way will discourage,
Christ will strengthen, comfort and encourage.
We will ask the Lord, what we should do.
His divine interest, He will renew.
As believers together, we bow and worship.
We are drawn to each other in fellowship.

In the harvest field, we labor.
Put God first and love your neighbor.
His kingdom we want to enlarge,
Submit to His will; let God be in charge.
Together, with the Lord, we labor in the field.
A bountiful harvest, we can expect to yield.
Negative speaking makes us an obstruction.
We will dutifully heed to the Lord's construction.
He guides our steps and we will not be downcast.
We live the abundant life and in the
Lord we stand fast.

The Greatest Possible Ascent

"And He said, 'Take now thy son, thine only son, Isaac, whom thou lovest, and get thee into the land of Moriah; and offer him there for a burnt offering upon one of the mountains which I will tell thee of.'"

GENESIS 22:2

Lord, we ask You for direction.
You are the Master of perfection.
The path to follow, God puts before us.
He asks us to walk in it; He implores us.
Our living Lord is ever-present.
He gives us a boast in our ascent.
To meet with God in prayer is expedient.
When He says now, we must be obedient.
His commands, do not abuse.
Follow Him; make no excuse.

If we choose His way, we will not be annoyed.
Decision delayed can be decision destroyed.
His way, we will choose.
In Him, we cannot lose.
Our wise, loving God will direct the test.
We know that in Him, we can rest.
Evil deeds could harmfully impact our future.
In difficult times, we must be on guard, for sure.
Christ redeemed us from sin; salvation is provided.
He paid the price in full; we will, by Him, be guided.

The Splendor of Transformation

"Therefore if any man be in Christ, he is a new creature: old things are passed away; behold, all things are become new."

II CORINTHIANS 5:17

As new creatures, in Christ, our lives are altered.
When trusting in self, we have faltered.
In Christ, all things have become new.
We no longer do the things we used to do.
A Christian has an outstanding feature.
His life is changed; he is a new creature.
Sin and darkness have lost their power.
We've been set free; He gives life this hour.
As a new creature, in Christ, the Spirit rules.
Love is one of His greatest tools.

He makes all things new.
His grace avails; to His commands be true.
We are changed from our selfish attitude,
Live your life full of gratitude.
In the newness of life, in Christ, we revel.
By the Word we are fed; there is no room for the devil.
When we are saved,
our lives are magnificently altered.
We are set free; no more have we faltered.
Christ is Prophet, Priest and King; in Him we trust.
For His sake we're pardoned; belief is a must.

Fully Trust and Apply It

"I do not frustrate the grace of God: for if
righteousness come by the law,
then Christ is dead in vain."

GALATIANS 2:21

To the Lord Jesus, we are devoted,
His love has always been promoted.
He is all-wise, upright, pure and a perfect sacrifice.
Only Jesus Christ could pay the price.
Christ presents us faultless before the throne.
We're devoted to Him; we are His own.
Christ is the answer to all of our needs.
We will pray and trust as our Savior leads.
Full salvation, our Savior brings.
When we are devoted to Him; our spirit sings.

We walk in His favor; His Light illumines all around.
Only in His righteousness is the special Light found.
His way, we will choose.
In Him, we cannot lose.
Make my life a hymn of praise.
I will trust God fully all my days.
The Son of God gave His life for you and me.
He ensures us a life of victory.
On the Son of God we rely and it is Him we desire.
God's gracious gift of salvation
is a treasure to admire.

Supernatural Schemes

"And he said, 'Blessed be the LORD God of my
master Abraham, who hath not left destitute my
master of His mercy and His truth: I being in the way,
the Lord led me to the house of
my master's brethren.'"

GENESIS 24:27

A yielded vessel, let each Christian be.
God gives what is best for you and me.
His life, within, is a divine design.
From sin and sadness we resign.
We see God in every detail.
To Him be the glory; He will not fail.
The Lord will lead, for we are one.
Be forever faithful to the Son.
Lead us, O Lord, and guide us on the way.
He is walking right beside us every day.

He makes all things new,
To Him, we will be true.
We are changed from a selfish attitude.
We live our lives full of gratitude.
Follow His way.
Trust Him and pray.
When there is a conflict,
Self-interest, restrict.
In Him we live and move and have our being.
We resist the enemy and send him fleeing.

Don't Interfere; You May Defer

"Peter seeing Him saith to Jesus, 'Lord, and what
shall this man do?' Jesus saith unto him, 'If I will that
he tarry till I come, what is that to thee?
Follow thou Me.'"

JOHN 21:21, 22

Our goal and purpose is to bless.
The love of God, we will confess.
Sometimes tests may be severe.
We will trust in God and be sincere.
Spend time in prayer and be in one accord.
Submit your will and follow the Lord.
God gives each one a lesson to be learned.
We know that salvation cannot be earned.
In other lives, don't step over the border.
We would be interfering in God's order.

A saint, on God depends.
To intervene brings different ends.
We can count on the Lord to take care of our needs
We will trust in Him as the Holy Spirit leads.
On the Triune God, our thoughts are concentrated.
To do His will, we must be consecrated.
Believe in the risen Christ and proclaim so.
When guided by the Holy Spirit, let the blessings flow.
The steps of a good man are, by the Lord, directed.
He upholds us; the Word of God is respected.

Even Yet, Fighting the Flesh

"Whether therefore ye eat, or drink, or whatsoever ye
do, do all to the glory of God."

I CORINTHIANS 10:31

In everyday situations, God is revealed.
He heals all nations; glean in each field.
For the glory of God, each deed is done.
His grace is extended to everyone.
Love one another; trust God each day.
The love of God, we do display.
We strive not for honor, recognition or fame.
To glorify God will be our aim.
God's glory, He does reveal.
May others see Him as our ideal.

Worldly ways in us are ridden.
Keep not Christ's light hidden.
By the Word, we are informed.
In Christ, we are transformed.
At any cost, make God's commandments your goal.
Come to Him; trust Him and be made whole.
Where the spirit of the Lord is, there is freedom.
Reflect God's glory; don't be troublesome.
We will not be offensive and lead others to sin.
We are free in Christ; He gives us peace within.

The Everlasting Aim in Life

"And said, 'By Myself have I sworn,' saith the LORD, 'for because thou hast done this thing, and hast not withheld thy son, thine only son: that in blessing I will bless thee, and in multiplying I will multiply thy seed as the stars of the heaven, and as the sand which is upon the sea shore; and thy seed shall possess the gate of his enemies;'"

GENESIS 22:16, 17

As we bless others, Christ blesses us.
Make Him your goal and make no fuss.
At any cost, on His path, He will lead.
We trust, and He fulfills our need.
Obedience to God is a must.
Come; let go; simply trust.
God will lead us to His goal.
We will love Him with heart, mind and soul.
God's promises are in Him; they are yea and amen.
We believe the Lord will come again.

We look to God and make our plea.
Our thoughts and actions must agree.
Yes, it is true, in Christ.
Promises are kept; He has sufficed.
In Christ, our goals are clear and He has provided.
Work together with Him and be not divided.
Life's goals are patterned to God's design.
The resources are abundant, each life to refine.
The Gospel hope is our anchor in this world's storms.
Set affections on things above; our Lord transforms.

Victorious Emancipation

"If the Son therefore shall make you free, ye shall be
free indeed."

JOHN 8:36

A new person, in Christ, is set free.
He is our individuality.
How great it is to be free in the Spirit.
He speaks the Word and we will hear it.
To commit and practice sin is to be a slave.
The Son liberates and helps us to behave.
Walk not after the flesh, but after the Spirit.
Flee sinful ways and don't come near it.
With Christ, our Savior, we are united.
He freely gives; we are delighted.

To launch our faith, we must be obedient.
His grace we will embrace; that is expedient.
Don't trust in a worldly form.
God's Word is to be our norm.
The Word is the fuel, and the Spirit, the flame.
Purposefully emit His light, in Jesus' name.
We go forth in obedience and God gives the grace.
He enables us to meet each task that we face.
Spiritual progress, by the promise, is measured.
His blessing is upon us;
each opportunity is treasured.

At the Time that He Approaches

"And when He is come, He will reprove the world of
sin, and of righteousness, and of judgment:"

JOHN 16:8

The basis of forgiveness is the cross.
To gain the world is to suffer loss.
Our debt of sin is paid in full.
The grace He gives is bountiful
On the tree, He paid the price.
He was the supreme sacrifice.
Through His shed blood, we are redeemed.
Jesus, our Savior, is esteemed.
We need not be filled with sin and remorse.
Come to Jesus; He is our source.

In Christ, we are forever free,
Heaven is our destiny.
Rebellion against God is a given fact.
Christ died on the cross, forever, the most loving act.
God has put Christians into a new position.
Our old nature is passed;
we have Christ's disposition.
The Spirit of truth, does righteousness reveal.
Upon the life of each saint, He has stamped His seal.
Worship the Lord, perpetually, in spirit and reality.
The soul's mirror reflects Christ's personality.

The Pardon is Through the Cross

"In whom we have redemption through His blood, the
forgiveness of sins, according to the riches
of His grace;"

EPHESIANS 1:7

God hates the sins of a sinner.
Carry the cross of Christ; be a winner.
Christ paid the debt of sin on the cross.
Know no defeat; suffer no loss.
He shed His blood; He did redeem.
He saves and keeps; Christ, we esteem.
On the tree, He paid the price.
He was the supreme sacrifice.
Through His shed blood we are set free.
Jesus, our Savior, gives victory.

We need not be filled with sin and remorse.
Come to Jesus; He is our source.
In Christ, we are forever free.
Heaven is our destiny.
Christ is the source of our redemption and life.
In the Father, Son, and Spirit, we are freed from strife.
Live for His glory and give praise from your heart.
A glorious inheritance awaits saints who are set apart.
As we observe with anticipation, we see Jesus only.
He is raised indeed; let not your heart be lonely.

Emancipated, Through the Cross

"I have glorified thee on the earth: I have finished the
work which thou gavest Me to do."

JOHN 17:4

Eternal life, God does bequeath.
It was accomplished by Christ's death.
From the cross, Jesus said it was finished.
His holiness is not diminished.
The sin of man, by God, is hated.
Only in Christ are we emancipated.
Christ's sacrifice was in God's plan.
He shed His blood for sinful man.
Believers are no longer, by sin, enslaved.
Through His grace we can all be saved.

The debt has been paid;
it is a blood-bought treasure.
Rejoice in the Lord; He is our pleasure.
In Christ we are able to rest,
When by the world, we are put to a test.
Jesus is exalted as Savior because of His sacrifice.
We have lives of joy and a promise of paradise.
God hates the wrong in sinful man.
Christ completed the work; it was the Father's plan.
God protects us from all the evils that lurk.
To God be the glory; Christ finished the work.

Superficial and Intellectually Deep

"Whether therefore ye eat, or drink, or whatsoever ye
do, do all to the glory of God."

I CORINTHIANS 10:31

We rest in the Lord and refuse to flaunt.
Each breath we take is significant.
Our precious walk with Jesus is ordained.
By doing all for His glory, we are not disdained.
Whatever we do, God has a part.
Life has a purpose, with Christ in our heart.
Jesus is with us in our walk.
He is in our daily tasks and in our daily talk.
Remember, the disciple is not above his Master.
To trust all to self leads to disaster.

Each moment, each day,
Let God lead the way.
Moment by moment, we have blessed communion.
There could be no more perfect union.
Each little thing we do can bring about results.
Our lives speak to others in whispers, not tumults
Step by step, with the Lord, we march on.
He knows every detail of life's marathon.
Allow not morals that are low to cause others to sin.
To combat wrongful attitudes, we need Jesus within.

Distinguish Clearly the Opposition

"Have mercy upon us O LORD, have mercy upon us:
for we are exceedingly filled with contempt."

PSALMS 123:3

Be not bogged down with useless cares.
The cares of the world ensnares.
The spiritual pathway is, by the flesh, opposed.
By our temper, selfish nature is exposed.
As the Spirit discerns, let us intercede.
Trust God to meet others, in their need.
The world wants to rant, rave, and riot,
God bestows, on us, His quiet.
Mistakes we make can be corrected.
Our lives are, by Christ, directed.

Let our eyes and thoughts, on the Lord, be fixed.
With worldly ways they may not be mixed.
With Him, we talk.
With Him, we walk.
By contempt, be not distracted.
Look to Jesus; to Him be attracted.
From sinful ways, make us exempt.
No longer will we have contempt.
Many scorn and scoff, knowing not of God's love.
Our eyes look to the Lord,
enthroned in heaven above.

Guidance of the Holy Spirit

"Behold, as the eyes of servants look unto the hand of their masters, and as the eyes of a maiden unto the hand of her mistress; so our eyes wait upon the LORD our God, until that He have mercy upon us."

PSALMS 123:2

On God, our Father, we rely.
His directions we won't deny.
Upon the Lord, our eyes will wait,
What He wills, He does relate.
Be not attached to any worldly alliance.
Upon the Lord, our God, is full reliance.
Look to the Lord and wait for His perfect direction.
Sometimes our thoughts will need correction.
We have a desire for something higher.
In Christ, we can be a worldly-pleasure denier.

In God's glory, we will revel.
We know that Christ defeats the devil.
It is our Heavenly Father that we serve.
From His path, we will not swerve.
We look to the Lord and are inspired.
Complete commitment is required.
Our efforts are high, because the Lord will aid.
Goals are accomplished; our pathway has been laid.
Rely not on what is worldly opinion.
God is our purpose for living; He has dominion.

Private, Unworldly Consistency

"But God forbid that I should glory, save in the cross of our Lord Jesus Christ, by whom the world is crucified unto me, and I unto the world."

GALATIANS 6:14

In the Lord, we are rooted and grounded.
On the cross of Christ, our faith is founded.
The cross is the center of what we believe.
Our trust is in Him; salvation, receive.
All have sinned; this cannot be denied.
Christ cleanses from sin; He was crucified.
Lift high the cross and don't be fooled.
Sin and darkness are over-ruled.
Trust not in dogmas and creeds and in ritual.
Spread the Word; it brings renewal.

Our thoughts and our eyes, on the Lord, are fixed.
With worldly ways, may they not be mixed.
Of this, we must be insistent.
Life in Christ must be consistent
When we love the cross, new energy is released.
New life, in Christ, frees us and we are pleased.
In Christ, alone, we are satisfied.
We are freed from doubt and fully gratified.
Sowing to the lower nature reaps decay and ruin.
Be a blessing to others; our Lord is coming soon.

Fixing the Mind on His Vital Power

"For in Christ Jesus neither circumcision availeth anything, nor uncircumcision, but a new creature."

GALATIANS 6:15

Go out and teach the world about Jesus.
His resurrected life will please us.
It is important for us to realize:
On the Lord, we must keep our eyes.
From worldly pleasures, turn away.
The living Christ will be our stay.
To know the power of the resurrection,
Jesus, alone, is our protection.
Trust fully in the One that was crucified,
With the Holy Spirit, be identified.

Jesus died and rose again.
In Him, new life does begin.
With the Word of God at the center,
Jesus Christ is our mentor.
We must focus on the cross and what it does mean.
Through Christ, our hearts are washed clean.
We want to have a healthy spiritual well-being.
Life, in the Spirit, must be at the center of our seeing.
We must set our minds on higher things.
Christ is our life; what a splendor He brings.

Dedication of His Vital Power

"Be not deceived; God is not mocked: for whatsoever
a man soweth, that shall he also reap. For he that
soweth to his flesh shall of the flesh reap corruption;
but he that soweth to the Spirit shall of the Spirit reap
life everlasting."

GALATIANS 6:7, 8

On Christ, the Lamb of God, we ponder.
From His truth, we will not wander.
Our life's ambitions, to God, are consecrated,
The way of the world is not highly rated.
As we walk with Jesus, He protects us from evil.
His deepest thoughts, He will instill.
What avails is to become a new creature.
A crucified flesh is an outstanding feature
In the cross of Christ we boast.
Draw near to Him; He is our Host.

We do not live a life of greed.
Our Lord supplies our every need.
Many gorge themselves with lots of stuff.
In Him, we surely have enough.
The Lord keeps us from the evil one.
We are dedicated to God, the Son.
Joy stems from within and not in earthly pleasure.
In Him, we are satisfied; He is our treasure.
Resort not to boastful comparison with your neighbor.
God's Word instructs; go into the fields to labor.

The Generosity of the Needy

"Being justified freely by His grace through the
redemption that is in Christ Jesus:"

ROMANS 3:24

Works won't get us to heaven; accept His Gift.
Jesus Christ is the Way to a spiritual lift.
God makes it clear; He is resolute.
Salvation is for the destitute.
Being poor in spirit is of no disgrace.
We are freely justified by grace.
We, in the flesh, deserve no merit.
But in Christ, the kingdom we inherit.
By the grace of God we are freely justified.
Redeemed, through Christ, we have testified.

We rest in God's amazing grace.
We need Him in each trial we face.
By grace we are freed.
Christ, alone, is our need.
The gift of salvation is for the deprived.
Christ avails; in Him, we've survived.
What is beyond our reach, has come to live within.
Heaven is in our hearts; Christ frees us from sin.
He desires that we think wisely and, of Him, inquire.
Redemption in Christ Jesus is what God does require.

Jesus Christ is Pure

"He shall glorify Me: for he shall receive of Mine, and
shall shew it unto you."

JOHN 16:14

The work, wrought by Christ is certain.
The cross of Christ is where we begin.
To glorify Him, be born anew.
Jesus Christ will live in you.
The Spirit of truth glorifies the Son,
God is the Blessed, Holy, Three-in-One.
The Savior, to us, has great appeal.
The Holy Spirit has been sent to reveal.
Jesus Christ is, to us, absolute.
Spread His light and share His truth.

When there is a need, we will go through it.
Give it to God, and He will do it.
Jesus Christ is supreme.
He, alone, is our theme.
In our lives, Lord, be glorified each day.
We joyfully exalt our Lord as we pray.
Of this we are resolute:
Our faith in Christ is absolute.
God guides us; step by step He shows us how.
Our freedom prevails in the here and now.

In Him, I Am Complete

"But by the grace of God I am what I am: and His grace which was bestowed upon me was not in vain; but I laboured more abundantly than they all: yet not I, but the grace of God which was with me."

I CORINTHIANS 15:10

Christ enables; He saves and sanctifies.
Be a yielded vessel; His grace He amplifies.
For each endeavor that we face,
God supplies His amazing grace.
On God's full mercy, is our reliance.
We are sanctified; make no defiance.
His grace, bestowed, is not in vain.
In His abiding love, we will remain.
When we say we are not able, we insult Him.
We can do all things. We will exalt Him.

Use and perfect the gift God has given you.
Bless those around you in every avenue.
We will bless the Lord all the time.
He is the One who is sublime.
We have not a will of defiance.
Upon the Lord, we must have reliance.
Give to God your very best.
Enter into the Sabbath rest.
My heart is glad and my body rests confidently.
He confesses us before the
Father's throne, providently.

December

For unto us a child is born, unto us a son is given: and the government shall be upon His shoulder: and His name shall be called Wonderful, Counselor, The mighty God, The everlasting Father, The Prince of Peace.
Isaiah 9:6

The Mosaic Code and Glad Tidings

"For whosoever shall keep the whole law, and yet
offend in one point, he is guilty of all."

JAMES 2:10

In the forefront of our minds, we keep the moral law.
The cross of Christ enables us with awe.
Christ has redeemed us, once and for all.
Without Him, we are sure to fall.
The law dictates absolute morality.
God's grace frees us from legality.
In God's love and mercy, we need not fear.
Reckon sin dead and, to Christ, adhere.
Jesus died to free us from sin.
We are thankful to be cleansed within.

We need not sit around and mope.
In the cross of Christ, there is always hope.
All have sinned and, of glory, fallen short.
The shed blood of Christ does sin abort.
God's demand is a life of moral purity.
Only in Christ, do we have security.
We are no longer condemned,
for Christ has set us free.
We are free of guilt and regret and live in victory.
Bear no grudges, but let love be foremost.
As children of God, in Him, be engrossed

A Disciple's Excellence in Christ

"Not as though I had already attained, either were already perfect: but I follow after, if that I may apprehend that for which also I am apprehended of Christ Jesus."

PHILIPPIANS 3:12

The aim of God is to make us one.
We are joined together with the Son.
A personal relationship to Christ is vital.
He lives within and that is our recital.
Nothing of this world is gain.
In Christ, we must remain.
Worldly pleasures are sometimes abused.
O Lord, lead us to where we are, by You, used.
Jesus Christ is our perfection.
He, alone, will pass inspection.

Forget the past.
Life, in Christ, will last.
Keep pressing on towards the goal.
God gives us strength and makes us whole.
We will read the Word and from its pages learn.
Christ is our perfection; for His presence we yearn.
It is only in Christ that we can excel.
The body is His temple; there, He will dwell.
Toward the heavenly prize, He calls us upward.
Await His coming; the trumpet will be heard.

Do Not Force; Rely on the Spirit

"And my speech and my preaching was not with
enticing words of man's wisdom, but in demonstration
of the Spirit and of power:"

I CORINTHIANS 2:4

In confessing faith, faith is renewed.
Redemption is proclaimed; reality is reviewed.
The power of redemption, we will not deny.
On the Holy Spirit, we will rely.
The Almighty God demonstrates His power.
He meets our needs this very hour.
It is not by might, nor by power, but by the Spirit.
We are sanctified by the Word; be sure you hear it.
By faith in God, be rooted and grounded.
Redemption is through Christ;
on this, faith is founded.

Read and study the Word;
it is worth more than gold.
No greater message can ever be told.
With the message of God's endearing love,
be instilled.
With the power of God, by the Spirit, we are filled.
With Christ at the center, we must testify.
Present the Gospel; the Holy Spirit will certify.
In Christ is God's power and God's wisdom.
From glory to glory more like Jesus we become.
Let our motives be pure; teach the message of grace.
Thank the Lord; we triumph in battles we face.

Action in Opposition

"He that hath an ear, let him hear what the Spirit saith unto the churches; to him that overcometh will I give to eat of the tree of life, which is in the midst of the paradise of God."

REVELATION 2:7

Life can be a battle for survival.
In our hearts, we need revival.
We, on this earth, must realize,
There are many painful times when we agonize.
When we are met with opposition,
God's grace will be our set position.
There will be a conflict to be endured with virtue.
Be renewed in the Spirit and immorality undo.
Remain faithful to Christ to the very end.
In Him, we overcome; He is our Friend.

With worldly wisdom, do not flirt.
To the Spirit, be alert.
Feast on the Word and learn.
The Holy Spirit will discern.
It is dangerous to just drift along.
Always remember that to Christ we belong.
We must not be adrift on the sea.
We must be strengthened daily morally.
We must accept His gracious invitation.
Salvation is through Christ; make no hesitation.

He Abides Within

"Thou shalt be over my house, and according unto thy word shall all my people be ruled: only in the throne will I be greater than thou."

GENESIS 41:40

Great is the Lord who sits on the throne.
My body, His temple, by His grace alone.
He gave His life to save our soul.
He is Lord; we are made whole.
The grace of God is absolute.
With Him, we will not dispute.
Within my body, the Spirit resides.
Ask Him in prayer and the answer He decides.
The salvation of Jesus is done forever.
I am saved; He will leave me never.

May the glory of God be fully revealed.
This can be done when, with the Spirit,
we are sealed.
Oh Lord, take complete control.
Cleanse our hearts and make us whole.
Our authority is in Christ; in His behalf act.
Our body is His temple and His purpose is exact.
The saint has his body under God's command.
Our thoughts and desires fit His purpose as planned.
With reverence and submission we worship the King.
Bow before His throne; high praises sing.

A Token of a Covenant

"I do set My bow in the cloud, and it shall be for a
token of a covenant between Me
and the earth."

GENESIS 9:13

Redemption is a finished work; it is done.
What is left for us is to accept the Son.
He paid the price, but we must enter in.
Look unto Him; He saves from sin.
For His mercy, we are forever grateful.
The bow in the cloud tells us that God is faithful.
God's great blessings are plentiful and complete.
We have sweet communion as we sit at His feet.
We live for His pleasure.
The Lord is our treasure.

The love of God is evident,
We are trusting; He is provident.
We can rest in confidence with the covenant signed.
Christ shed His blood and our lives are refined.
We know the reason why God
set a rainbow in the sky.
We are blessed by the covenant
and on the Word rely.
The Lord's understanding is beyond measure.
The blessings He bestows we will treasure.
Faith gains victory over unbelief and we press on.
Christ's righteousness justifies; the battle is won.

Godly Sorrow for Evil

"For Godly sorrow worketh repentance to salvation
not to be repented of: but the sorrow of the world
worketh death."

II CORINTHIANS 7:10

When we sin, it makes God sad.
True repentance makes us glad.
Sorrow for sin should be genuine.
It helps us to begin again.
It is necessary to tell the Lord we are sorry.
It is then that we catch a glimpse of glory.
For this the Son of God was sent;
What is expected is that we repent.
Turn away from sin or there will be sorrow.
Do it today and do not wait until tomorrow.

The Word of God will bless; we will share it.
Turn to Christ; salvation, through Him, we will merit.
Expect release from all your past mistakes.
Happy is the one who sin and evil forsakes.
True repentance causes us to turn around.
Leave sin behind and be heaven-bound.
Go away from evil and do what is pure.
Victory, through Christ, He does ensure.
Stay away from evil influences; they tend to defile.
God comforts and encourages; that is His style.

The Unprejudiced Authority of God

"For by one offering he hath perfected forever them
that are sanctified."

HEBREWS 10:14

Full salvation is for all.
He paid the debt; on Him we call.
He paid the price upon the tree.
He gives His joy and victory.
The way of the cross, we will proclaim.
We are washed in the blood; praise Jesus' name.
Full pardon is received through Christ's death.
His resurrected life, He does bequeath.
The Lord puts before us many an opportunity.
Be servants of righteousness in your community.

Redemption through the blood has sufficed.
We find love and peace and joy in Christ.
We cannot earn salvation; for us, His blood was shed.
The tears we shed in sorrow are tears of joy, instead.
Complete provision, on the Cross, was provided.
Salvation avails; evil's reign has subsided
Resist worldly passions; salvation profess.
When sin is committed, we must confess.
We will not forget what the Lord commands.
We are safe and secure when in His hands.

Displeasure of the Flesh

"And they that are Christ's have crucified the flesh
with the affections and lusts."

GALATIANS 5:24

Human selfishness must expire.
A life, in Christ, will truly inspire.
What we do in the flesh does not avail.
When we want the credit, we are sure to fail.
What is noble, right, and good is our choice.
When we depend upon Christ, we will rejoice.
Our sinful nature has been crucified.
New life, in Christ, will not be denied.
Prayer is important; talk to God more and more.
Great things are done, when Christ we adore.

Daily, our devotion we give.
Die to self and, in Christ, live.
The life once lived, we now oppose.
Life in Christ is what we chose.
Our lives are made spiritual by sacrifice.
Renew your commitment; that is great advice.
On one another, we show concern for each friend.
We build together in Christ; on Him we depend.
The Lord is our Helper; we will not be alarmed.
In Him we have confidence and are fully armed.

The Sacrifice of the Flesh

"For it is written, that Abraham had two sons, the one by a bondmaid, the other by a freewoman."

GALATIANS 4:22

Jesus, our Lord, was crucified.
In Him, we are truly sanctified.
Our natural flesh must be transformed.
Obey, in the Spirit, and be reformed.
Present yourself as a living sacrifice.
The Spirit's orders are precise.
What happens to us is in God's permissive will.
When we walk in the Spirit, His life He will instill.
Through God, flows the water of life.
When we yield to Him, He suppresses strife.

With satan, make no compromise.
Walk in the Spirit, with no disguise.
Keep alive the Lord's glorious wonder.
We want hearts that grow fonder
New life in Christ is what we will nourish.
It is then that good fruit will flourish.
The world, the flesh and the
enemy are forever teasing.
We must walk in the Spirit to be God pleasing.
Our commission is to tell others the Good News.
Each one we encounter has a pathway to choose.

Distinct Existence

"Then said Jesus unto His disciples, 'If any man will come after Me, let him deny himself, and take up his cross, and follow Me.'"

MATTHEW 16:24

Our selfish ways, we will deny.
Only the Lord, will satisfy.
It is human nature to go one's own way.
Lord, lead us by Your will, as we walk each day.
Let no bitterness afflict your heart.
Mend your ways and get a new start.
The enemy is on the prowl and wants to pick a fight.
We will follow Jesus with all our might.
We may sometimes suffer ridicule.
We grow in grace, when in His school.

As disciples, self we deny.
On the Holy Spirit, we rely.
With fame and fortune we have flirted.
It is then that we are self-asserted.
It is not right to have resentment.
When we walk in love, we have contentment.
Our desire is to do His will; the Spirit does discern.
No deceptions will stand; for the truth we yearn.
May sinful ways and worldly lusts be eradicated.
May our lives be sanctified and wholly dedicated.

One, with the Son

"And the glory which thou gavest Me I have given
them; that they may be one, even as we are One:"

John 17:22

The Creator understands us fully.
We are at peace with Him; walk gracefully.
Jesus prayed that we be one.
Be merged with Him and call it done.
It is the Lord who really understands.
He is our Creator, and He holds us in His hands.
Our Lord desires that we be of united heart,
From His precepts never part.
How can we improve our personality?
Be devoted to Christ; trust His ability.

With Christ, we are of one accord.
Our lives reflect the Son, our Lord.
We are no longer lonely;
We seek Jesus only.
With love, through Christ, we are transformed.
We reflect His glory; new life is formed.
The slightest sin, the Spirit will detect.
From evil thoughts and actions, He will protect.
To be sanctified wholly is to be,
by the truth, separated.
God protects from evil; we are emancipated.

What Is That In Your Path? Pray!

"And He spake a parable unto them to this end, that
men ought always to pray and not to faint;"

LUKE 18:1

When we meet someone in need,
We should at first intercede.
Keep on praying and persevere.
Trust God to lead you and be sincere.
Each day, we may meet someone new.
Pray to the Lord, that their faith He will renew.
Prayer releases and gives protection.
Our eyes are opened to each detection.
Press on toward the goal and don't give up.
He has made us whole; drink from His cup.

When there is a need, lend a helping hand.
With prayer and praise we will take our stand.
May the words we speak be God approved.
By the Holy Spirit, we are moved.
Pray with purpose, persistence and power.
Peace and assurance, on us, He will shower.
Be completely open unto God and have no regret.
Hold your loved one in prayer, until their need is met.
We will not lose heart and we will not turn back.
God defends and protects us; in Him is no lack.

Simple Trust

"Peace I leave with you, My peace I give unto you;
not as the world giveth, give I unto you. Let not your
heart be troubled, neither let it be afraid."

JOHN 14:27

On You, O Lord, we will completely rely.
Your peace and mercy, we can't deny.
God has promised His peace.
When we obey, our cares He will ease.
Let go of that which is perverse.
Difficulties will reverse.
Do not be troubled or afraid.
The Lord delights when we have obeyed.
We should never try to serve two masters.
Obedience to God keeps us from disasters.

Christ is our peace.
He gives sweet release.
Strive not, of this world, to conform.
Perfect peace becomes our norm.
In the midst of difficulties, we are freed.
In each situation, trust God to meet the need.
We are no longer, from God, far away.
Christ is within; He has come to stay.
A heart full of sin, will be very unsettled.
Listen not to what the evil one has peddled.

Sanctified to Jehovah

"Study to show thyself approved unto God, a
workman that needeth not to be ashamed, rightly
dividing the Word of truth."

II TIMOTHY 2:15

To ourselves and others, we will express,
God's compassion, when there is distress.
Oh Lord, help us to state what is on our heart.
From Your truth, we will not depart.
Sincerely give and pass it on.
To the Word, they will be drawn.
Study the scriptures and you will understand.
Pray, fast and worship, and hold His hand.
God is faithful to His Word; He is loyal.
Remain in His comfort; our Lord is royal.

It is God that we seek.
It is His Word that we speak.
To speak the Word, prepare.
It is best to start with prayer.
May the words we speak be, by God, approved.
By the Holy Spirit, we are moved.
Rehearse words to express God's truth clearly.
Let all you meet know that you love God sincerely.
Sinful actions lead to God's
judgment and displeasure.
Ask for God's wisdom; He will bless beyond measure.

Contrary to God's Will?

"Wherefore take unto you the whole armor of God,
that ye may be able to withstand in the evil day, and
having done all, to stand…Praying always with all
prayer and supplication in the Spirit, and watching
thereunto with all perseverance and supplication for
all saints;"

EPHESIANS 6:13, 18

We are complete in Christ; He answers prayer.
Wear His armor; victory share.
In prayer and in witness, we are on the Lord's side.
Always, forever, in Him abide.
Wrestle against opposing forces.
Do only what the Lord endorses.
Work with God; make prayer intense.
Spiritual victories He will dispense.
With worldly ways, continue to wrestle.
Lord, make us into a useful vessel.

The battle is best fought,
When first the Lord is sought.
In Christ, we are complete.
No longer, for our own self-will, compete.
With worldly ways, we put up a fight.
Stand firm in the Word and fight for the right.
We will more than conquerors be.
We will march on to victory.
To trust in man, we meet with despair.
The Lord imparts wisdom and loving care.

Deliverance is Supplied

"But the natural man receiveth not the things of the
Spirit of God; for they are foolishness unto him:
neither can he know them, because they are
spiritually discerned."

I CORINTHIANS 2:14

The god of this world strives to poison our mind.
We need redemption; seek the Lord and find.
The Creator satisfies the need.
Unto the Word, will we give heed.
Redemption creates and satisfies.
Our desire for Christ intensifies.
Rely not on human reasoning and emotion.
Be equipped with the Spirit and
have faithful devotion.
The Word of God brings conviction and healing.
The inner thoughts of the heart, He's revealing.

Richly, in us, Christ does dwell.
By our words and actions, we will tell.
Those who do not believe are blinded.
Be born again to be spiritually minded.
Unbelievers cannot understand nor see.
We must love and share Christ's love continually.
The blind may hide behind many masks.
God may not give until someone asks.
The Lord is our Helper; in peril, He brings relief.
We are consecrated by our faith and belief.

The Critical Exam of Faithfulness

"For I am persuaded, that neither death, nor life, nor angels , nor principalities, nor powers, nor things present, nor things to come, nor height, nor depth, nor any other creature, shall be able to separate us from the love of God, which is in Christ Jesus our Lord."

ROMANS 8:38, 39

God puts circumstances into place.
Praise Him in each trial you face.
God has a plan, but we have faltered.
Sometimes our plans must be altered.
To the Lord, we will be true.
Look to Him; He will renew.
God will work all things out for good.
We will know and do whatever we should.
How does the Lord, our lives, enhance?
He controls each circumstance.

We are ready Lord, for Your command.
On the Word of God, we stand.
We love God; He works for our good.
According to His purpose, He said He would.
We are under the Sovereign King's care.
He gives what is best, His blessings, to share.
To God's call, we must be obedient.
We are available; this is expedient.
In Him is constant communion.
Faith is a victorious union.

Devoted to His Peace

"Think not that I am come to send peace on earth: I
came not to send peace, but a sword."

MATTHEW 10:34

Rebuke that which is wrong.
It is to God that we belong.
From God, we can keep no secrets.
When we try to, we will have regrets.
Grace and peace are His reward.
To fight the battles, we need His sword.
The happiness that the world promotes is a fake.
True joy comes for Jesus' sake.
The battle is on; the sword is our weapon.
The Word of God makes the warrior a champion.

When dealing with the insurgent,
The Word of God will be most urgent.
Be not filled with selfishness and pride.
It is in Christ that we must abide.
The Lord is our Helper; we will not be alarmed.
We are confident that we will not be harmed.
God is on the throne, His works are anointed.
What a blessing it is to be divinely appointed.
Our earthly goods will be left behind.
Treasures in heaven, we will find.

Only To the Cross

"And I, if I be lifted up from the earth, will draw
all men unto Me."

John 12:32

All the lost, in this world, have an unending need.
Come to the cross and to Christ give heed.
God judges the sins of men; He is fair.
We are cleansed by the blood; this we declare.
Our mission is to lift up Jesus.
He is the only one who can free us.
Earthly gain will suffer loss.
To be rich, lift up the cross.
God helps us; our hearts, He is changing.
Through Christ, our lives are rearranging.

The world is in turmoil.
We need the Holy Spirit's oil.
The prince of this world is to be cast out.
Christ is lifted up, without a doubt.
Not I, but Christ be lifted high.
He, alone, can sanctify.
Diligently seek the Lord and a rich reward acquire.
He is Master of our heart; the Spirit will inspire.
It is the Lord, Himself, who gives us grace.
The Holy Spirit's power we embrace.

Personal Trial or God's Disclosure

"Now we have received, not the spirit of the world,
but the spirit which is of God; that we might know the
things that are freely given to us of God."

I CORINTHIANS 2:12

The source of redemption is Christ.
Being freely born again; He has sufficed.
Our lives have been born new; that is real.
The Holy Spirit, within, will be our zeal.
A productive life has Jesus as its source.
What bears fruit is what He will endorse.
A worthwhile experience has Christ at the center.
It is through the cross that the redeemed may enter.
We have faith; in God we can be sure.
He gives us hope that does endure.

He is the Word; trust Him alone.
He came; for our sins, He did atone.
Jesus is God's Word revealed.
Trust in Him and, to Him, yield.
The Spirit searches the things of God that are deep.
We have the mind of Christ; a watch He does keep.
Experiences sometimes make us enthused.
Be sure, by them, you are not confused.
God's counsel we respect; He has made us aware.
We will walk in love; the full Gospel we will share.

Attraction of His Deity

"No man can come to Me, except the Father which hath sent Me draw him: and I will raise him up at the last day."

JOHN 6:44

God speaks; let us hear His voice.
To do His will is our choice.
Jesus calls us; His love does instill.
When we believe, we want to do His will.
To God, our Savior, we are drawn.
He is the One we can depend upon.
The Father draws us unto Him.
His way is bright; it won't grow dim.
It is our yearning to believe.
In Christ is life and Him, we receive.

Our desire to delight in the Lord is growing.
It is great to remember, He is all knowing.
To believe is our will.
Trust in Him to fulfill.
The Father draws us to the Son.
When we believe and receive, our hearts are won.
In God, we are confident.
The joy He gives is evident.
He was tempted and yet He did not sin.
Receive and welcome Him; trust His power within.

In Christ, We Are Reconciled

"But God forbid that I should glory, save in the cross
of our Lord Jesus Christ, by whom the world is
crucified unto me, and I unto the world."

GALATIANS 6:14

We are indeed dead to sin.
The Lord Jesus Christ lives within.
In the cross of Christ we glory.
That is the message of the Gospel story.
The penalty for sin was paid upon the cross.
Any other way, will mean our loss.
Our old nature, with the Lord, is crucified.
He has changed our lives; we have testified.
No longer do we sit in our selfish prison.
Our hearts rejoice for He has risen!

The Lord Jesus Christ was crucified.
With His meaningful life, we are identified.
In Christ, what avails is a new creature.
Live for His glory; He is the divine Teacher.
We will acknowledge Him as Lord, with persistence.
To be like Jesus, is the life-line of our existence.
Live in peace; let not bitterness defile.
The Lord is faithful; agree to reconcile.
Christ is our High Priest and His promises bless.
With His heart and mind, true faith we confess.

Hide in Christ

"For ye are dead, and your life is hid
with Christ in God."

COLOSSIANS 3:3

A yielded life, to God, is secure.
He guides each step and makes us pure.
We are safe when we walk in the light.
He directs us and keeps our footsteps right.
Apart from God our life is precarious.
As we abide in Him, we are victorious.
Become born again, and lift your voice in song.
Christ lives within and to Him we belong.
To a life set apart, the Spirit has bidden.
With Christ, in God, your life is hidden.

Stand firm in your faith; life's struggles are strong.
It is a comfort to know, to Christ we belong.
In Christ, our lives are full of grace.
He expands His forgiveness to all human race.
Put off the old man and his deeds.
Wisdom from the Word fulfills our needs.
The best gift we can give is our life.
When fully yielded, we can live above strife.
Our new lives in Christ are purified.
Shameful lives and acts of sins are to be denied.

Christ is Born: We are Born Again

"Therefore the Lord Himself shall give you a sign;
'behold, a virgin shall conceive, and bear a Son, and
shall call His name Immanuel.'"

ISAIAH 7:14

God is with us; He is Immanuel, the Son.
He came to give His mercy to everyone.
As we yield to Jesus, in us,
His likeness will be formed.
To the world, we will no longer be conformed.
In lowly esteem, He came from on high.
His nature avails to those who draw nigh.
Through Christ, God, in the flesh was manifest.
He offers to us His peace and rest.
Our Savior's birth was a miraculous day.
From heaven to earth He came, the sacrifice to pay.

In Christ, we are born anew.
He came, our lives and spirits to renew.
This could be our last day, month, week or year.
No one knows when He again will appear.
The virgin conceived; a sign had been given.
God provided a Lamb, that we be forgiven.
In the majesty of the Lord's name, we are secure.
He is our only peace; it is a peace that will endure.
Jesus said, "I and My Father are One."
We are born of God and the victory is won.

Identify with the Radiant Jesus

"But if we walk in the light, as He is in the light, we have fellowship one with another, and the blood of Jesus Christ His Son cleanseth us from all sin."

I JOHN 1:7

Christ's blood that was shed cleanses.
God's forgiveness, He dispenses.
Christ has placed His perfection within.
His atonement washes away our sin.
Walk in the light and experience His grace.
Have intimate fellowship, in each time and place.
By the blood of Christ, we are continually purified.
Trust in His finished work, that He be glorified.
We are attracted to the light.
The love of God puts sin to flight.

While on this earth, we will endure each test.
Bask in His light and choose what is best.
There is no darkness in God; He is light.
His path is straight and His ways are right.
With the radiant Jesus, we identify.
The works of the evil one, we defy.
We are of the truth; assurance needs no retreat.
His good work in us will continue and be complete.
God can make a permanent home in your heart.
From His precepts we need never depart.

Defeat or Victory

"For thus saith the LORD to the men of Judah and Jerusalem, 'Break up your fallow ground, and sow not among thorns.'"

JEREMIAH 4:3

The battle is fought with forces unseen.
Only the blood of Jesus can keep us clean.
God is always on our side; we will win.
The battle is the Lord's; let it begin.
We must meet with God in the secret place.
He will then give us victory, in each battle we face.
We can be certain that the conflict will be won.
God is with us, a constant companion.
Precious times are spent with God, alone.
The Spirit releases; may His power be shown.

For God's glory, we exist.
To do His will, we persist.
We meet God, in prayer, in the secret place.
It is there that the Lord, we do embrace.
We fail, if we choose to go our own way.
Return to the Lord; let Him be your stay.
Believe and do His will, His glory to exemplify.
Our time upon the earth quickly passes by.
May sinful ways and worldly lusts be eradicated.
To the Lord, we are sanctified and dedicated.

Uninterrupted Transformation

"And said, 'Verily, I say unto you, Except ye be
converted, and become as little children, ye shall not
enter into the kingdom of heaven.'"

MATTHEW 18:3

Put on the new man and His likeness.
Without Him, our spirit is lifeless.
We must turn to God each new day.
He alone, can show us the way.
Humble yourself, as a little child.
We are easily molded, when meek and mild.
Turn away from all that is wrong.
Communion is required; to Him, we belong.
To our worldly ways, we must not revert.
God must rule; He does convert.

In Christ be formed.
Become transformed.
Day by day our lives are changed.
We grow in grace as God arranged.
Offend not the little child that believes.
Know that the humble, the kingdom receives.
We are changed, to His likeness, from glory to glory.
Each day is new; proclaim the Gospel story.
Love and forgive is God's command.
On the sacred truth we stand.

Leaver or Cleaver

"Then said Jesus unto the twelve,
'Will ye also go away?'"

JOHN 6:67

Oh, Lord, Your Word I will cherish.
Without the vision, the people perish.
Worldly possessions must not prevail
God's heavenly vision will not fail.
The truth of the Word is proclaimed,
Jesus is Lord and this is acclaimed.
It is a delight to walk with Him and obey.
It is not what we own, but what we are day by day.
The test that we face sometimes will frighten.
The truth sets free and does enlighten.

Lord, show us the way.
Help us to obey.
In Christ, there is no lack.
We will not turn back.
When the Father calls us, we need to come.
New life, in Christ, is not cumbersome.
Follow Him and do what He commands.
We are safe when we are in His hands.
Christ Jesus was sent to bless us;
we look for no other.
As children of God, He leads each sister and brother.

In Christ, His Pure Morals, We Partake

"As well the singers as the players on instruments
shall be there: all my springs are in thee."

PSALMS 87:7

Life at its best, in Christ, is manifest,
It is then that our old nature is suppressed.
Draw from the springs of living water.
Be yielded vessels to our Heavenly Potter.
Our selfish ways won't accomplish much.
To the Spirit, we must keep in touch.
The past is forgiven and we are made new.
In Christ, we take on a spiritual view.
As we make music, we will play and sing.
Living waters, the Spirit will bring.

With righteous garments, we are clad.
We are transformed; in Christ, we are glad.
Living waters will flow out.
With joy we will praise and shout.
Sing songs of Zion and worship the King.
Speak glorious things, glad tidings to bring.
God has a cure for sin's pollution.
The cleansing blood of Jesus is the solution.
Our source of joy is in Zion, the city of God.
We will speak of its splendor, as on earth, we trod.

History is His Story

"For ye shall not go out with haste, nor go by flight:
for the LORD will go before you; and the God of Israel
will be your reward."

ISAIAH 52:12

Be not anxious about the past.
We are being prepared for things that last.
We cannot control what has been done.
God leads us on; His race is run.
Our future is yet to be explored,
The God of Israel will be our reward.
We will follow His purpose and plan.
Salvation avails today for every man.
Look not back on the race you have run.
Victory is ahead; shout with praise; we've won!

Keep moving forward and don't look back.
Remember, in Christ, there is no lack.
In Zion, the LORD forever reigns!
His kingship is over all domains.
The enemy's goal is to be destructive.
With God's help, we will be productive.
There is a spiritual blessing of prayer and praise.
We are a living sanctuary; God does amaze.
The Light of the world, our path does make bright.
He gives us great joy and helps us to do right!

CPSIA information can be obtained
at www.ICGtesting.com
Printed in the USA
LVHW091159061118
596086LV00031B/75/P